HANDBOOK OF

HORARY
ASTROLOGY

Karen Hamaker-Zondag

SAMUEL WEISER, INC.

York Beach, Maine

To Henny M. van den Bor, in friendship

First published in 1993 by
Samuel Weiser, Inc.
Box 612
York Beach, Maine 03910

Library of Congress Cataloging-in-Publication Data

Hamaker-Zondag, Karen.
    [Handboek voor uurhoekastrologie. English]
    Handbook of horary astrology / by Karen Hamaker-Zondag.
        p.   cm.
    Translation of: Handboek voor uurhoekastrologie.
    Includes bibliographical references and index.
    1. Horary astrology.   I. Title
    BF1717.5.H3513 1993
    133.5'6--dc20   92–1761
                                                              CIP
ISBN 0–87728–664–7
MV

Translated by *Transcript, Ltd.*, Wales

Typeset in 10 point Garamond

Cover painting copyright © 1993 Ananda Kurt Pilz. Used by kind
permission of the Walter Holl Agency, Germany.

Charts used in this book have been calculated and printed by Astrolabe, Inc. of Brewster, MA, using its *Nova* and *Printwheels* computer
programs.

Printed in the United States of America

The paper used in this publication meets the minimum requirements
of the American National Standard for Permanence of Paper for
Printed Library Materials Z39.48–1984.

Table of Contents

List of Charts

Foreword

Horary astrology is an old art and has its own set of rules which are not hard to follow, although they do call for the development of a certain degree of skill. In this book, I have tried as systematically as possible to state these rules, together with their exceptions and any associated problems. I have illustrated them with a number of real-life examples. Horary astrology lends itself to questions about common everyday situations, so there are plenty of examples we can use for practice.

Horary astrology is in the process of being rediscovered, just as character astrology is developing, though its development is not so vigorous as that of modern psychological astrology. I have tried to pay due attention to this in the chapters on generally neglected subjects such as the link between horary and natal charts, and the link between horary charts and personal progressions.

A moment's reflection should persuade us that, if the birth chart does not concur, there is no point in believing a horary chart that says we could become famous film stars. A disagreement of this sort should not arise often because experience shows that horary charts keep surprisingly in line with the trends of the natal horoscope and — to revert to our example — the chances are that if the latter dashes our hopes of stardom, so will the former!

Now, where the relationship with one's own chart is concerned, there are several points of interest: such as why events take place at one time of day and not another, and why the querent poses a question at a certain instant. In fact we need to learn the value of the apparently unimportant moment when someone asks us to cast a horoscope. Horary charts provide unexpected information that can add precision to progressions; and, if we use them, these charts will give guidance through life. Many horary charts seem to be related to each other and to the radix. Once we realize what this means, we shall no longer regard horary astrology as a simple yes/no technique, but as an instrument for uncovering hidden connections between ourselves and the life that goes on around us — a real adventure! I hope that in this book readers will find the information needed to help them look for the hidden connections in their own lives.

Some cases involve primary directions or secondary progressions, or transits. Astrologers are in agreement over the secondary progressions and transits, but have some differences over primary directions.

The method employed here is the one devised and thoroughly tested by Wim van Dam. This method has always given extremely satisfactory results in my own practice. The house system it uses is that of Placidus, the system I have always found best.

My special thanks go to Anneke and Carolien, both of whom supplied their horoscopes and agreed to the publication of these together with their circumstances, as examples of the relationship between horary charts, the birth chart and personal progressions. And, of course, my thanks are also due to my husband Hans who read through the manuscript as usual, improving it in numerous places and offering constructive criticism.

Karen M. Hamaker-Zondag

1

What is Horary Astrology?

Horary astrology is much older than the character-reading form of astrology. Its rules are also much more black and white than are those of the modern psychological approach. In character reading, a planetary position is open to different interpretations and offers a number of different development possibilities, while in horary astrology the same position is taken as an unequivocal yes or no. Although horary astrology has clear rules for passing judgment, it is still an art, for even these simple rules have their exceptions, and there are contradictions that have to be weighed against one another. Horary astrology often offers clear-cut answers to questions; but, if a single rule is overlooked, those answers can be completely false.

Its black and white character and explicitness have made horary a favorite form of astrology, and it was once very popular.

There are different kinds of horary charts, all of them derived from oracular astrology. As far as we can tell, mundane astrology is the oldest form of astrology, used mainly to foresee and predict the destinies of nations and rulers. In mundane astrology, a big part was played (and still is played) by such things as eclipses of the Sun and Moon, conjunctions of Jupiter and Saturn, and the like. In today's psychological astrology, these tend to be pushed into the background.

How and when mundane astrology arose is not known. Probably, it goes back to primeval times, when humans did not look at natural phenomena in a rational, logical way, but experienced them inwardly. We felt that everything around us was animated, and we projected spirits and souls onto various material objects. We believed in tree spirits, ancestral spirits, the spirit of the Sun, and so on. The Sun and Moon were seen as dispensers of light that banished the terrors of darkness. But the Moon regularly withdrew, and sometimes (when new) ceased to be visible. She became invested with a mystical air which she retained until people saw that her waxing and waning were regular, and learned how to use the cycle. Naturally, solar and lunar eclipses preyed on the imagination and caused great anxiety when the spirits of darkness won a victory over the light!

In that conceptual world, Sun, Moon and Stars were seen as Great Spirits; and worship of the Moon, in particular, was widespread. Perhaps treating their rhythms as part and parcel of daily life is the oldest form of astrology; but it seems to have little in common with astrology as we know it.

However, as human beings gained an increasingly clear idea of solar and lunar cycles, and discovered such rhythms in nature as the changing seasons, the emphasis shifted from the worship of the "mysterious heavenly bodies" to their use in planning such activities as agriculture. This new development called for the framing of a calendar based on some astronomical measure of time. At first this measure was taken from the Moon. Devising a calendar presupposes two abilities: first, the development of the art of writing and second, the prolonged observation of the starry sky. Therefore calendar construction can be practiced only by people with special training—by priests for example, as was the case in ancient Egypt.

The way in which temples (used as astronomical observatories) and priests were associated with knowledge of the heavens, no doubt encouraged belief in the divinity of the stars; especially as calendars were developed not only for agricultural purposes but also for fixing the dates of religious ceremonies and festivals. Many nations—such as the ancient Egyptians, the ancient Chinese, the Aztecs and the Mayans—popularly regarded the calendar as the *Book of Fate*.

In Babylonia, however, it was thought that the gods gave signs and omens through particular arrangements of the heavenly bodies. In contrast to *calendar* interpretation (which attaches a fixed meaning to fixed units of time, such as days), it was the changing pattern of the sky that was important there. So that which occurred with regularity—that which continually altered—was felt to express the divine will. In order to discover the will of the gods from all these unexpected formations, everything that went on in the sky was carefully recorded side by side with all the accompanying events on earth. For the first time, reasonable conformities were collected on the principle of "as above so below." That we are so well informed about Babylonian practice is due to the fact that in 1847, in the area of the ruins of Nineveh, more than twenty-five thousand small cuneiform clay tablets were excavated from the library of King Assurbanipal (669–626 B.C.). Four thousand of these clay tablets contained portents and predictions.

Elsewhere in the world, too, a study was being made of the relationship between constellations in the heavens and happenings on earth. Astronomy and astrology were still indissolubly linked. A clay tablet of 419 B.C. carries the earliest mention we have of all twelve signs.[1] Consideration of the movements of the planets and stars led to the discovery of rhythms and cycles, and this produced a big leap forward (especially) in the sixth century B.C., making it possible to calculate—in advance—the positions of the Moon and those of the five known planets. The familiar division of the zodiac into equal 30° parts as an indispensable unit of measurement also seems to have been made around this time.

This period also witnessed the first split between astronomers and astrologers. However, astrology did not die out, although it did undergo some far-reaching changes, changing more and more, and falling in and out of favor, until we come to how we use it today. The following list briefly explains the various kinds of astrological techniques that have developed out of oracular astrology over the years:

• *Event Charts*—This involves the erection of a chart for the time and place of some occurrence such as a wedding, a proposal, the launching of a ship, the start of a quarrel, the beginning of an electioneering campaign, and so on. The chart provides an insight into how things will turn out.

• *Electional Charts*—Here a horoscope is cast in advance in order to find the best possible moment for something important; for example, the

---

[1]From Wilhelm Knappick, *Geschichte der Astrologie*, p. 39.

signing of a contract, the founding of a society, the solemnization of a marriage (the pronouncing of the "I do"), and so on.

• *Political Charts*—The charts of countries and politically significant events such as the signing of peace treaties, the promulgation of decrees, etc.

• *The Consultation Chart*—An unjustly neglected horary technique that delivers good results and is a valuable tool for the professional astrologer. A chart is erected for the moment the client enters the office. From this chart, we can read not only his or her current situation, but also developments in the near future.

The basic rules considered for the charts mentioned above are more or less the same. There are a few differences in approach; but these will be explained where necessary.

The Horary Chart

A horary chart is an ordinary horoscope for which the usual information is needed—the date, place, and moment of the event or inquiry. The asking of the question is a separate technique, which will be discussed in detail in the following chapter. We must impress on ourselves that without posing a proper question it is not possible to receive a proper answer. Of course, some sort of answer will be received if the rules set out in later chapters are applied; but the rules are not reliable unless the question is clear and to the point.

As we shall see, the houses play a key role in the answering of questions, so I will dwell on them first. Experienced astrologers may safely skip the rest of this chapter.

The horoscope is divided into twelve zodiac signs and twelve houses (or areas of life). The houses are usually of unequal size. Their relative sizes differ according to the time and to the degree of latitude where we find ourselves. The starting point of a house is called the cusp. So we speak of cusp 2, cusp 5 and cusp 9 when referring to the precise starting points of the 2nd, 5th and 9th houses respectively. The Ascendant is in fact cusp 1 and the Midheaven or MC (Medium Coeli) is cusp 10.

Each cusp falls in a certain sign. Sometimes there will be signs with several cusps, and sometimes signs with none at all. This is something else that depends on the time and on the geographical degree of latitude. The sign containing a cusp is important, because that sign is associated with a planet known as the ruler or dispositor of the sign.

A house cusp is ruled by the ruler of the sign it occupies. It does not matter if the house itself overlaps another sign; what is decisive is where the starting point, or cusp, of the house falls. Say Gemini is on cusp 6 and part of Cancer also lies in the 6th house; Mercury, as ruler of Gemini, will be sole ruler of the house.

In horary astrology, all the information is based on rulers. If this is forgotten, the answer fails. So it is a good idea to memorize the planets and signs that belong together. (See Table 1 on p. 6.) There is a lot of disagreement about day and night rulers. Many students of astrology start doing horary charts after they have worked with character analysis, and are used to looking at the chart from a personal point of view. It is important to see the difference between interpreting a horary chart and a natal chart. Although there are many different systems, and some horary specialists would disagree, the system that we use in Holland is quite simple. We use as the day-ruler of a sign, the planet that is the most important ruler of that sign. For example, Saturn rules Capricorn, and is the most important ruler of the energy. The night ruler of the sign would be the less important planet. For Capricorn, it would be the newer planet, Uranus.[2]

To determine the house ruler, simply look in the day ruler column. The planet mentioned there is the principal ruler of the sign. The night ruler is subsidiary to the day ruler. If different from either, they tend not to be used in the analysis unless they are trans-Saturnian planets. In horary astrology, many practitioners still prefer to confine themselves to

---

[2]Readers should also note that in the traditional scheme provided on page 104 of William Lilly's classical work on horary astrology (*Christian Astrology*, London 1659), Leo has the Sun as both day and night ruler, and Cancer has the Moon as both day and night ruler. The other signs have either a day or a night ruler; not both as listed in Table 1. The traditional scheme works by alternating the day houses with the night houses; thus, if one sign is a day house, the next sign is a night house, the next a day house, and so on. Aries comes first, and is the day house of Mars; this means Capricorn works out as the night house of Saturn, and Aquarius as the day house of Saturn. But, according to the author, Capricorn has Saturn as its day ruler and Aquarius has Saturn as its night ruler. The difference is probably caused by fitting the newer planets into an old scheme. Students of horary may want to explore both systems. Trans. note.

Table 1. Signs and their Day and Night Rulers.

Signs	Day Ruler	Night Ruler	Classic Ruler
Aries ♈	Mars ♂	Pluto ♇	Mars ♂
Taurus ♉	Venus ♀	Venus ♀	Venus ♀
Gemini ♊	Mercury ☿	Mercury ☿	Mercury ☿
Cancer ♋	Moon ☽	Moon ☽	Moon ☽
Leo ♌	Sun ☉	Sun ☉	Sun ☉
Virgo ♍	Mercury ☿	Mercury ☿	Mercury ☿
Libra ♎	Venus ♀	Venus ♀	Venus ♀
Scorpio ♏	Pluto ♇	Mars ♂	Mars ♂
Sagittarius ♐	Jupiter ♃	Neptune ♆	Jupiter ♃
Capricorn ♑	Saturn ♄	Uranus ♅	Saturn ♄
Aquarius ♒	Uranus ♅	Saturn ♄	Saturn ♄
Pisces ♓	Neptune ♆	Jupiter ♃	Jupiter ♃

the Sun, Moon and the classical planets (Mercury, Venus, Mars, Jupiter, and Saturn). They substitute Mars for Pluto in Scorpio, Saturn for Uranus in Aquarius, and Jupiter for Neptune in Pisces. This point will be considered in detail in chapter 5.

When you study horary astrology, you must understand that there is a problem between traditional horary astrologers and more modern students. Very traditional astrologers don't want to consider the outer planets in a horary chart. Modern horary astrologers are open to consider their possible use. I must say that I stand in-between; I am convinced, purely by experience, that the old or classic rulers do work without any problem. But in the case of a question about pilots or engineers, I find that with Aquarius rising in a horary chart that I can also use Uranus as the ruler of the 1st house without altering the outcome of the chart. So I have had some indication that we astrologers have to expand the horary theory because we live in different and changing times. This will evoke a lot of resistance from the traditional horary astrologers. I advise students to use the classic rulers, but to also be open to experiment with the outer planets as rulers as well. This is what makes horary astrology exciting!

In dealing with house rulers and their houses, it is of the utmost importance to know precisely under which planet, which sign or which house a person or object should be categorized. On this, the interpretation of the horary chart stands or falls! In doubtful cases, *The Rulership Book* by Rex Bills can prove very helpful.

2

The
Question
or Event

There should be no difficulty in erecting a horary chart, because the method is exactly the same as the one used for a natal chart. In fact, the moment a question is asked or an event occurs can be treated as the "birth" of that question or event. So the calculation is straightforward. What can be a problem, however, is the asking of the question. Therefore we need to know what is and what is not allowable.

The wording of the question itself should be as direct, as plain and as simple as possible. Once it has been formulated, the question must be written down on paper and *not changed afterward*. If someone asks a question in an unclear way, we must try to define the problem precisely before proceeding to erect the chart; because a muddled question will receive an equally muddled answer.

Should we suddenly think of another question while calculating, drawing or interpreting the chart, we must erect an entirely new horary chart for this question, even if it has to do with the first question. Each question has its own moment. If we ignore this point, we shall land ourselves in hopeless difficulties when we come to interpretation.

Another problem that may arise is that although the question has been clearly formulated, it is not the right question. Now and again we shall find that, for some reason or other, people are too timid or afraid to mention the real problem, and therefore ask indirect or evasive questions in the hope of receiving an answer to what is on their mind. It will be obvious that, in such a case, the horary chart will present the astrologer with a very confused, and even misleading, picture, and that the querent will certainly not obtain an answer to the unspoken query. When matters are like this, it is often better to say that the chart is not straightforward enough to interpret, rather than to try to figure out the real question.

Sometimes (fortunately not always!) disreputable motives make the astrologer's position awkward. Thus someone once asked the perfectly legitimate question, "Am I named as heir in the will of X?" Normally, the horary chart would enable us to answer yes or no to such a question. But in this instance there were conflicting indications, some of them centering on Neptune. Certain of the indications were positive, but one or two were very problematical. As it turned out, the question asked was not the real question. The inquirer had already pocketed a generous helping of the inheritance, and was simply hoping that this would not be found out. The positive indications showed that there was indeed money or property, but the negative indications referred to the dishonesty surrounding the situation and the question. However, a conflicting horary chart by no means always implies deceit on the part of the querent, so it will always remain a headache in interpretation.

Very general questions are also impossible to answer by means of a horary chart. We need a concrete and clear-cut area or subject. A further limitation is that of time; for a horary chart has only a limited period of validity, as we shall see later. If we make a general inquiry along the lines of "Shall I have a happy life?" (a question that crops up quite often!), the vagueness will be repaid either by a meaningless answer or by no answer at all. But if we ask, "Would it be good for me to accept that offer?" then we have a very clearly defined starting point which should make the horary chart possible to interpret.

On the whole, questions in the style of, "Will there be another World War?" are also too general. They are impersonal and have to do with large groups, and we shall find that it is hard to make them fit into a horary chart. But a question such as, "We are on the verge of war, am I likely to be called up and sent to the front?" is possible to answer quite easily, since it is focused on a concrete situation affecting one person.

A further complication occurs when the querent asks the astrologer a question about a third party. Some astrologers refuse to deal with such questions, which have a way of making horary charts difficult to handle. However, always bearing in mind the importance of doing nothing that could be construed as unethical or an invasion of privacy, it is certainly possible to answer questions about third parties by means of horary astrology. But we do need to know in which house of the chart this person is shown, and we also need to be very careful in deriving our answer. Horary astrology works best with questions when they are about ourselves or about the person making the inquiry.

One should never repeat the same question within a short space of time! The first chart is the only one that counts, the others are valueless. To be sure, we can ask the question again if various things have happened to alter the situation or bring about fresh developments. Then a supplementary chart can be prepared. But the general rule is that a question may not be asked more than once.

What is the best mode of expression for our question? This depends on the sort of answer we wish to obtain. If all we want is a yes or no, the question can be cast in this form: "Shall I sell my house soon?" "Shall I get a bank loan or not?" "Will my lost dog come home?" and so on.

A horary chart can also be used to gain insight into a situation, in order to find out the whys and wherefores of a thing and to draw conclusions from it. If that is our intention, then it is better to word the question like this: "What would come of writing such and such a letter?" "What opportunities will open up for me when I have finished my studies?" or "What would my prospects be if I agreed to a business merger with firm 'X'?"

Also with problems of choice, a horary chart can help. For example, we can ask questions of the form: "Doctor A says this and Doctor B says that. Whose advice should I take?" "Is it better for me to accept this job or to finish my studies first before starting work?"

Even though the horary chart covers a fairly restricted field, has its limitations and is fairly black and white, we can nevertheless use it where there are psychological problems. It can reveal what lies behind them, and can even help in the choice of therapy should the need arise. Although horary charts are still hardly ever used for this purpose, we can in fact ask all sorts of questions such as: "What would be the result of going to psychiatrist C?" "What type of occupation would be good for my condition?" "Is all I need a fun holiday and a chance to unwind, or is there something more serious the matter with me requiring professional attention?" "Should I go in for group therapy, or would individual therapy be better?" Any question of this kind can be answered by means of a horary chart.

In short, we need to fulfill the following requirements:

• Word the question as clearly as possible;

• Once it is written down, do not change it;

• Ask a given question only once. If it is necessary to repeat it, do not do so before several months have elapsed and fresh developments have taken place;

• Do not ask general questions;

•, Ask straightforward questions, not concealed ones;

• Be careful with inquiries about third parties.

We need to be thoroughly aware of the fact that the interpretation largely stands or falls with the question!

What is the Moment of the Birth of the Question?

When does a question lend itself to treatment by the horary method? For although the wording of the question is important for interpretation, the moment the question is asked determines the chart pattern on which interpretation is based. When someone else puts a question to us or gives us a piece of information, the vital moment is the one when we heard the question, received the letter, and so on. But precision is less easy to attain if the question is our own and has been bothering us on and off. Seldom can we state precisely when a problem began; and this makes it difficult to erect the horary chart. The best thing to do is what many astrologers do, which is to adopt the moment when it first forcibly struck us that we had a problem in need of a solution. We have all experienced occasions when we suddenly realized the full extent and consequences of some matter. A moment like this is suitable for a horary chart.

But we do need to play fair. Astrological practitioners have been known to "cheat" by deliberately calculating a favorable moment for the answer to some question (this is not easy to do, incidentally), and then phoning that question to an astrologer friend. The start of the call is then used as the moment for which the chart is erected, and the chart is used as the basis for working out developments. From experiments conducted by others and myself, it has emerged that these little tricks are futile and lead nowhere. Planning horary charts do not make for valid horary charts—they simply don't work. This means that the factor of spontaneity plays a big part. Only if a question occurs naturally can an informative horary chart be read.

To clarify this situation, the time the horary question is asked clearly, and the astrologer understands it, is the time I use in horary astrology. Many clients have called me with the question: "Can I ask you a question?" And I reply, "Yes, but please put the question to me as clearly as possible. If you don't feel able to do so, please describe the situation and the problem, so that we can deduce the question." Many clients ask their questions straight away, so there is no time problem. But there are those who are unable to formulate the question so that it can be asked of a horary chart—very often because their circumstances are quite complicated. These clients start describing the whole situation. Most often it turns out that the moment that they start to describe the problem is the right time for the horary chart. But if a client calls, and halfway through the phone call he or she suddenly says that he or she wants to ask this question of a horary chart, then I take the moment that he or she actually asks the question in the middle of the conversation. So different situations are possible, and students will have to explore these possibilities.

In regard to the factor of spontaneity, Joan Tittsworth gives an example of a question asked during her lessons by one of her students. Horary charts for missing persons were being discussed, and this student had a brother whose whereabouts had been unknown for more than twenty-five years. Of course, when the subject came up, the student thought of his brother and asked, "Is my brother still alive?" 0°15' Gemini was on the Ascendant, an indication in horary technique that the chart is not capable of being judged correctly (see chapter 3). Tittsworth says that this result must be attributed to the fact that the question did not occur directly or spontaneously, but was prompted by an extraneous factor (the lessons). Tittsworth calls the question "forced." However, my own experiments with questions prompted in this manner frequently produced charts containing helpful information. Sometimes extraneous factors can suddenly turn a vague question into one that is clear and topical. It doesn't really matter what makes the question emerge so definitely; the fact that it does emerge definitely is what is important.

A book on horary astrology will often suggest to students a whole series of questions on the subjects it mentions. I myself have found that charts prepared for these questions are safe to interpret. Readers might want to conduct their own tests with questions that occur to them while they are studying. Simply note the date, place, and time of each question, and see if the answer makes sense and also if it turns out to be correct. Through experiments of this sort we learn how to best handle such questions.

If we have to deal with a question from another person, we should note the moment the question was asked. Practical experience justifies this completely. Astrologers usually erect the chart for the place where the question was asked; in most instances this is the place where they have their office. One or two astrologers prefer to erect the chart for the domicile of the client; which can give rise to problems when the client casually rings up, not from home, but from a distant part of the country or from abroad. Although there is something to be said for taking the location of the client as our starting point, it is also perfectly satisfactory to calculate horary charts based on the location of the astrologer. Sometimes, however, the horary chart for the client's place of residence differs considerably from the chart for the astrologer's office; even to the extent that, while one chart is hard to judge, the other is not. So far, my experiences have not given me a settled preference for either type; although it does seem to me that the Ascendant of a horary chart erected for the place from which the client phones the question, is more likely to make an exact aspect with some planet in the client's birth chart. Readers are advised to experiment to see which method gives them the best results, always bearing in mind the following points:

• When erecting a chart for someone else, use the moment the question was asked;

• When erecting a chart for yourself, use the moment the question became crystal clear to you;

• The place where you heard or thought of the question can always be used for the chart.

Finally, for an event, the rule is to use the moment the event began and the place where it occurred. We must be careful how our questions are framed! Suppose a civil disturbance has broken out somewhere and we know from reports exactly when the trouble started; if we wish to study the course of the disturbance, we must erect a chart for its time and place. But if what we really want to know is whether or not the disturbance will spread to where we live, possibly causing us harm, then it is better to ask a direct question and erect a horary chart for our own place of residence and for the time of the question (rather than for the time the disturbance started). The time, the place and the nature of the question are always closely connected!

How Long is a Horary Chart Valid?

When a horary chart gives a negative answer, we must not think that this "no" implies that what is being inquired about will never happen. The situation can alter, and new developments can occur to change the answer. One might suppose that these developments would show in the chart, but they do so to a very limited extent and only when they are due within a few months. Many horary astrologers allow for an average chart-life of three months, but we should not treat this as a hard-and-fast rule—considerable latitude is possible either way.

If the inquiry is very important or urgent as far as the querent is concerned, then an initial no can turn into a yes some months later. But, by the same token, the answer can again be negative. Thus, during periods when it is very difficult to sell one's house, horary specialists are frequently asked about the chances of a sale. I myself have known cases where the answer was no for several years in a row, and then there was a yes followed swiftly by the sale of the house.

A horary chart concerned with a single question is not valid for the whole life of the querent. All that a horary chart does is show us facets of the here-and-now and of the immediate future that springs from it, and then only for matters touched on by the question.

Just because a horary chart only lasts for a limited time, don't throw them away. There is quite a lot that can be done with them. A horary chart can be responsive to progressions and transits, and if we keep track of them, we shall make some surprising discoveries. Charts of questions and charts of events are equally valuable. Charts of events are sensitive to progressions over a fairly long term. For example, if we erect an event chart for the moment when a government takes office, a president is sworn in, a king or queen is crowned, or a firm is founded, we shall find that it is valid for the entire period that the government remains in power, the president heads the administration, the monarch reigns, the business flourishes, etc. And that is usually a good deal longer than the few months for which ordinary horary charts are valid.

Progressions and transits can be employed to determine times. But in horary astrology other techniques are also used to pinpoint dates of happenings related to the question. More will be said about these in chapter 7.

3

When
not to
Pass Judgment

According to tradition, there are some charts that are risky to interpret because they contain indications either that they can give no answer to the question, or that the querent or the astrologer will make mistakes. Sometimes, too, the question is no longer applicable. There can be many reasons why certain charts are impossible to interpret or can be interpreted only with the most extreme caution, quite apart from the fact that the wording of the question may be at fault.

The accepted wisdom is that we have to be on our guard in the following cases:

1. *When the Ascendant is in the first three degrees of a sign*. In a case like this, it is difficult to say anything, because the situation to which the question refers does not yet give us enough to go on. It is still too soon to be able to give an answer. Further developments must take place before the matter is ripe for a horary chart.

2. *When the Ascendant is in the last three degrees of a sign*. The last degrees are telling us that it is "too late." The situation has run on so long that there is little the querent can do. The die has been cast, the

decision has already been made, even though sentence may not yet have been passed. All the querent can do is to watch what happens.

3. *When Saturn is in the 7th house.* The querent is signified by the 1st house and the astrologer by the 7th. If Saturn is in the 7th house, this means that the astrologer is going to have problems—caused perhaps by an error in arithmetic, by a poorly drawn chart, by overlooking some factor that affects the interpretation or, given that none of the relevant factors has been missed, by a faulty assessment of their meaning. The experience of many astrologers definitely goes to show that such mistakes can occur when Saturn occupies the 7th house of a horary chart; so it is not a bad idea to be extra careful if that happens. Nevertheless, it has been found in practice that such a chart can be used effectively provided every precaution is taken.

If the astrologer is asking a question on his or her own behalf, the interpreter of the chart is now represented by the 1st house. Then, of course, it is Saturn in the 1st house that can cause problems.

Some horary astrologers mistrust not only all charts with Saturn in the 7th, but also all charts with Capricorn or Aquarius on the 7th cusp, since Saturn is the day dispositor of Capricorn and the night dispositor of Aquarius.[1] In other words, they view Saturn with suspicion just as much when it is the ruler of the 7th as when it is posited in the 7th. However, there is no general agreement on this, and in practice there is not enough evidence to convict Capricorn and Aquarius of being Saturn's accessories. In itself, the sign on this house cusp tells us nothing.

In any case, Saturn in the 7th is not always a drawback. When the 7th house represents the astrologer or the role of the astrologer, a Saturnine astrologer (one with the Sun, Moon or Ascendant in Capricorn, or with a powerfully placed Saturn, etc.) will not be inconvenienced by, what is to them, a compatible Saturn in the 7th.

Again, some questions have specifically to do with 7th-house situations (marriage, teamwork, open enemies, etc.), so we should not reject all charts with Saturn in the 7th as impossible or dangerous to interpret. This would imply that there were no Saturnine marriage partners, enemies, and the like—which is obviously ridiculous.

Traditionalists still lay great emphasis on the "bad" side of Saturn in the 7th but experience teaches that Saturn in this house need not

---

[1]Note that some astrologers will disagree with this rulership.

always be so troublesome. Caution is always advisable, but if we double-check the chart, see if we have overlooked such points as summer time, and pay extra attention to detail, that is probably sufficient. Usually we shall discover nothing more than some trifling fault or omission. The latest developments in horary astrology tend to confirm this. Of course, there are other possibilities: for example, the client pays scant attention to the astrologer, throws the latter's advice out of the window, or—and fortunately this rarely happens—the advice lands the astrologer in difficulties. Saturn is the planet of constraint, and astrologers who fail to abide by the moral and ethical constraints of the profession can stir up trouble for themselves—for instance, by offering medical advice they are not qualified to give. But astrologers who behave impeccably have nothing to fear in that respect from this position of Saturn.[2]

4. *When the Moon is void of course*. We say the Moon is void of course when she forms no further major aspects with other planets while she is still passing through the sign where she is. That is to say when she has made her last major aspect in her present sign and does nothing more until she enters the next. There are several interpretations of a Moon void of course (see chapter 6). As an impediment, it usually indicates that the querent will be unable to do anything about the answer received. A Moon void of course denies the possibility of taking action; events will unfold without the querent being able to intervene.

Yet there are times when it is very good to have a horary chart with a Moon void of course. For instance, when one is afraid of something. It assures us, as already said, that nothing is going to happen; therefore the thing dreaded will not happen.

5. *When the Moon or planet representing the querent or the quesited is in the Via Combusta*. This is a very old rule, and is no longer

---

[2] I have seen that Saturn in the 7th house can indicate trouble, but I have also experienced situations where that Saturn placement was no trouble at all. The danger that the astrologer may make a mistake is indicated here. I always calculate a chart with Saturn in the 7th more than once and study it twice before explaining it to my client. It may also point to troubles that the client will have with his or her partner or companion, so it can be useful in interpretation. Only in a few cases has what Lilly said come true, which is why I have not laid special emphasis on this position, or provided an example of it. Students will have to experiment with this placement to see how it works for them.

observed by all horary astrologers. The Via Combusta—The Burning way or Combust Way—is the section of the zodiac between 15° Libra and 15° Scorpio, except for 23° through 24° Libra. In olden days, the Via Combusta was reputed to be the most dangerous part of the twelve signs, owing to many violent fixed stars found there. But the stars are no longer in the same place relative to the signs, so modern astrologers ignore the rule. The exception of 23° Libra through 24° Libra is understandable—these are the degrees (in our present time) containing Spica and Arcturus, thought to be fortunate stars.

Looking at the matter objectively, there is not a single reason for clinging to the Via Combusta, and certainly not for deciding that a chart is incapable of being safely judged because of it. However, it must be mentioned that, guided by personal experience, the renowned horary specialist Barbara Watters did not completely abandon the Via Combusta rule. She found the effect to be similar to that of a Moon/Uranus conjunction, in which events take a sudden, unpredictable turn that is not always relished by the querent. She also found that frequently there is something compulsive and calamitous involved.

The fact that there is so little agreement on the rule, and that the majority of astrologers are inclined to throw it overboard, should serve as a warning to be very circumspect in its use. I myself have occasionally noticed something of the capriciousness reported by Barbara Watters, but at other times it was absent. Readers are advised to experiment and then make up their own minds on the subject.

One or two further remarks are needed on rules 1 and 2 (Ascendant in the first three and last three degrees of signs). These rules have their exceptions; but once again, alas, opinions are divided. However, the following is definitely true: if the Ascendant of the horary chart is in one of the first three or last three degrees of a sign, and if this degree is the same as the Ascending degree of the querent's radix (within a 1° orb), then, without doubt, the horary chart is ripe for interpretation. The reason for this is that the querent has asked the question at a very personal moment, the moment when the degree on his or her own Ascendant was rising. Often a question asked at this time will mean a great deal to the querent.

Another exception, which applies more especially to rule 2, is that when the inquirer is the same number of years old as there are degrees on the Ascendant, the chart is safe to judge. Of course, this exception applies only to those who are between 27 and 30. The same exception can also be made for rule 1 in respect of those who are 0 through 3 years of age, but one does not anticipate that anyone so young will come along with a question!

Rules 1 and 2 are not thought to apply when the Ascendant of the horary chart is within one degree of the inquirer's progressed Ascendant, or when the Ascendant of the horary chart is within one degree of a conjunction with a radical planet or point of the querent. Some astrologers have extended the latter exception to mean that if the horary chart's Ascendant is within one degree of a major aspect with a radical planet or point, the horary chart is still safe to judge. I myself have often had experiences that support them in this.

As we see, there is no complete unanimity on the subject of when a horary chart may and may not be interpreted. Those that are supposed not to be safe to judge do sometimes contain valuable information. We ought to make a special effort to learn by experience the art of getting around the various difficulties that present themselves. The important thing with all these rules is to proceed with caution!

The

Quesited — the person or thing about
which the question is asked

Querent (~~the~~ ~~ibn~~ _the inquirer_)

If someone comes to ~~me~~ with
a question about someone else, then
we will have to decide which house
represents the ~~other~~ third party

4

Derived
Houses

Suppose that, at a given moment, ten different questions are asked: one horary chart will have to answer them all. Now, it is highly unlikely that all ten answers will be affirmative or that all ten will be negative; so how can a single chart say yes to some questions and no to others? It can do so only if we use the technique of moving the houses around the chart, called deriving the houses.

Whenever we ask a question, it is essential to know which house represents the querent (the inquirer) and which house represents the quesited (the person or thing about which the question is asked). *The querent is always represented by the 1st house*. In other words, the 1st house describes the present condition of the querent. If we, as astrologers, ask a question on our own behalf, then we are represented by the 1st house in the same way. But, if a person comes to us with a question about someone else, then we have to decide which house represents this third party. For instance, if a mother asks a question about her child, the mother (as querent) is represented by the 1st house, and her child is represented by the 5th house of the horary chart, which is always the house of children. See figure 1 on page 22. If she wishes to make a specific inquiry then — say it concerns the health of her child — we must *not* consult the 6th house of the chart, for that has to do with the health of the querent herself. No, we must look for the house that

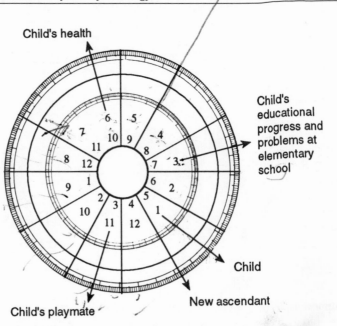

Figure 1. An illustration of the horary chart whereupon a mother asks about her child.

acts as 6th to the 5th, namely the 10th house. We find this by altering the houses as follows: having located the house that represents the individual (in this case the 5th house), we treat this as the 1st house (in our example, the 5th house has to be treated as the 1st house) and renumber the other houses accordingly. The old house meanings have to be changed, too. Thus the horary chart's 10th house has nothing to do with the social position of the child, but has become the child's 6th house and provides a certain amount of information about the child's state of health.

If the same mother wants to know something about the child's elementary schooling, we have to look at the 3rd to the 5th house, which is the 7th house of the horary chart. Or, if she is interested in how the child is getting on with its playmates, then the 11th to the 5th is taken, which is the 3rd house of the horary chart.

Now suppose the mother asks us a question about a child who is a family member, though not her own child, but a child of her husband's previous marriage. Then we must work with a completely different house than the one we used for her own child. This needs care. How do we proceed? Well, the child belongs to her husband, who is represented by the 7th house of the horary chart; therefore it will be represented by the 11th house, because that is 5th from the 7th. If we want to know something about that child's state of health, we use the 6th from the 5th from the 7th house. By simply counting around the horary chart (see figure 2 on page 24) we reach the 4th house of the chart, and this will provide us with information on the state of health of the stepchild. If we have one or more questions to ask concerning the child, we must treat the 11th house as the 1st house, and go on from there. Thus, learning problems would be found in the 3rd house from the 11th, and that is the 1st house of the original chart.

It will be clear that, if we do not identify the correct house for the question, the interpretation will be seriously affected, to say the least! It will also be clear by now that we can answer all sorts of questions with a horary chart, and that the answers can be varied. Imagine that the following questions are being asked at the same moment in the same place:

- My sister-in-law wants to sell her house. Will there be a quick sale?

- Is this the time to ask my employer for a raise?

- Will my holidays be trouble free?

- My dog has run away. Will he come back?

- My brother wants to start a business with X. Will the partnership be successful?

- I am in love with Y. Are we going to get married?

- My son-in-law wants to sue for money that is owing to him. Will he win?

Let us try and find the houses belonging to these questions. Which house represents a sister-in-law or brother-in-law? If these are the sister and brother of a spouse, then we use the 3rd house counting from our partner's house. The 7th house represents our partner, and the 3rd house counting from that represents our partner's brothers and sisters.

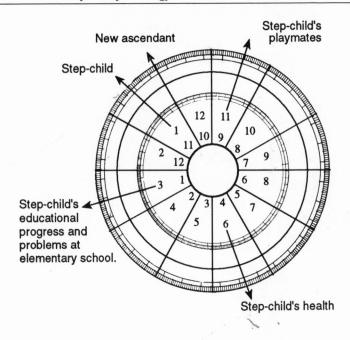

Figure 2. How to locate a step-child in the horary chart.

So in order to answer a question about the sister-in-law, we must treat the 9th house as a 1st house and proceed from there.

The question about the sister-in-law has to do with the sale of her house (for buying and selling see also chapter 11). Real estate comes under the 4th house, buyer and seller come under houses 1 and 7 respectively, and the 10th house is the negotiated price. Using house 9 (the sister-in-law) as our starting-point, we now locate the new 1st, 7th and 10th houses, and find that house 9 is the new 1st house, house 3 the new 7th house, and house 6 the new 10th house. The property itself is therefore in the old 12th house (new 4th) and the negotiated price in the old 6th house (new 10th). (See figure 3 on page 25.)

In the question about asking for a raise, the querent is represented by the 1st house. The employer is the 10th. To see if the employer can afford the raise, we treat the 10th house as the 1st because he or she is now the main subject. The employer's financial

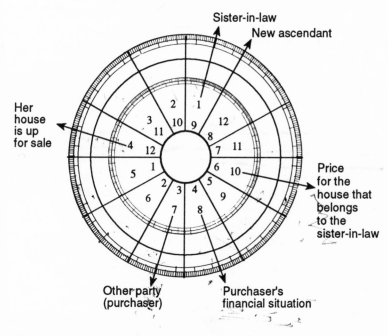

Figure 3. The horary chart for the sale of a house owned by the querent's sister-in-law.

situation lies in the 2nd house which, in the original chart, is the 2nd house to the 10th—in other words, the 11th.

For holidays we use the 9th house. Since we are considering the querent's own holiday, he is represented by the 1st house in the horary chart and no adjustment is necessary.

Inquiries concerning a lost dog are sometimes hard to answer. Everything depends on what the dog means to the querent. If it is a watchdog, it performs a useful function and so comes under the 6th house. But if it is a companion, or even a substitute for a child, then we can look at the 5th house. Thus, either house 5 or house 6 can be taken as the starting point for discovering what has become of the animal.

For questions about a brother or sister, the 3rd house is our starting point, and is treated as a new 1st house. If we want to know about some partnership he or she is considering, then we use the 7th house — as reckoned from the original 3rd house. This 7th house is house 9 in the original chart.

When the question is one of a possible marriage of the querent, we use the 7th house of the original chart without renumbering any of the houses. But the 5th house, the house of romances and the time before marriage, must also be taken into consideration as long as there is no cohabitation.

A son-in-law is a daughter's husband. One's own child is represented by the 5th house. The child's partner is represented by the 7th house to this, namely the 11th. Therefore the 11th house has to be treated as if it were the 1st when we want to know the result of the son-in-law's suit. The judge's decision lies in the new 10th house, or old 8th. In a lawsuit we always have the person or persons being sued, found (astrologically speaking) in the house of open enemies, the 7th. Calculating this from the 11th, we find that it is the old 5th house. Figure 4 shows how to read the outcome of a son-in-law's lawsuit.

A single horary chart has an almost inexhaustable capacity for answering different questions, because different questions involve different houses and chart connections. But we must observe the rule of *confining our attention to those significators and houses that have to do with the question*. The rest of the chart usually has no significance and therefore must not be considered in our answer.

When trying to find the house to which a certain person or thing belongs, we can sometimes run into problems. We have already seen that where a domestic animal is assigned (5th or 6th house) depends on what the animal means to the querent.[1] Points like this have to be decided *before* a question is answered. But there are other things that depend on the everyday world of the querent. For example, someone who moves around a lot in a job like that of trucker or traveling salesperson, will have a very different outlook from that of someone who grew up in a closed rural community and has never set foot outside it. For the traveler, a town sixty miles away is still just up the road; whereas, for the backwoodsman, a ten miles distant village can be another world. It is of the utmost importance to know what a

---

[1] William Lilly, *Christian Astrology*, p. 392 ff., in his chapter on "A Dog mising, where?" says, "The Sign of the sixt and his Lord signifies the Dogge; so must they have done if it had been a Sheep, or Sheep, Hogges, Conies, &c. or any small Cattle." Traditionally, dogs belong to the 6th (Lilly's sixt) house. Trans. note.

person experiences as "far away" and "nearby," before we answer any question about distance, that is to say any question involving the short-distance 3rd house or the long-distance 9th house. Objective measurements, expressed in miles for example, cannot be given for these houses.

The allocation of houses to the parents is a big problem, too. One group of astrologers places the mother in the 4th house and the father in the 10th house, another group does the precise opposite, and a third group makes no distinction but places the parents jointly in the 4th/10th house polarity. The last group appears to dodge the issue somewhat, but is actually in agreement with psychological reality. When it is a baby, the child does not experience its parents separately. It sees the father through the unconsciousness of the mother, so that there is no question of a difference between the parents. Only afterward does it become increasingly aware that there are two different parents, and that father and mother are each important in their own way. Because of that initial experience of unity during the most impor-

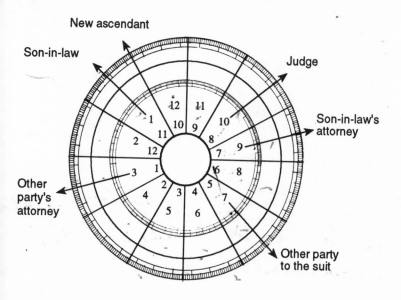

Figure 4. The same chart showing the houses involved when determining the outcome of a son-in-law's lawsuit.

tant phase, the phase in which most of the connections are made among the child's brain cells, there is no difference on which it can build later. So, how do we decide which houses best represent the parents? There are several possibilities. If both parents are still alive, and if the question concerns one of them, the chart itself nearly always gives us enough to go on. In many cases, we shall observe that the cusp of the 4th or 10th house is in the Sun Sign of one of the parents. Or the planets in one of these houses exactly represent the situation of the parent concerned. Or the Ascendant of the parent falls in the 4th or 10th house of the horary chart, etc. In practice, this frequently simplifies our choice, so that, in spite of theoretical difficulties, we know the house at which we ought to be looking. If there is only one surviving parent, he or she seems often to be represented by the 10th house; but even here there are exceptions.

One house in the horoscope serves as a kind of "last resort" for those who are hard to place. When in doubt, we can assign them to the 7th house. In general, the 7th house has to do with partnerships and companionships, with cooperative efforts, with open enemies and with those relationships that have a (positive or negative) emotional or practical value for us.

It is only natural for us to have difficulty with house meanings in the beginning. Sad to say, there are no rules to give for the numerous variations we can meet; the rich embroidery of life contains more patterns than can ever be covered by an author's examples and suggestions. This is why it makes sense to save our old horary charts—they have such good teaching value. By studying them in the light of further developments, we can see where any of our house attributions have been wrong, and what other factors we are liable to overlook.

The horary has a slight variation in time, color meaning etc than the Natal chart

5

First Steps
in
Interpretation

The interpretation of a horary chart differs in a number of vital points from the interpretation of a natal horoscope. The horary chart does not contain the nuances of the natal chart, and the picture it presents is much more black and white. To judge it correctly, we must always follow the standard set of basic rules. There are a number of refinements to these rules, and we shall come back to these in a later chapter.

When there is a question we want answered for ourselves or for someone else, and we have erected a horary chart for it, then we set to work as follows:

A. *See if the chart is safe to judge*. Examine whether the Ascendant is in the first three or last three degrees of a sign, or Saturn is in the 7th (when the question belongs to someone else) or in the 1st (when the question is our own), or the Moon is void of course or in the Via Combusta. If we find one or more of these limiting conditions, we must be very careful, for then the chart is much less reliable (see chapter 3). No risks must be taken with the interpretation and we must proceed with great caution.

If we find none of the above limitations, then we can continue without any more ado.

B.) *The querent is always signified by the 1st house and the Moon.* There are always planets that represent the querent, and these planets are known as *significators*. The most important of them is the ruler of the 1st house, or Lord of the Ascendant. Planets in the 1st house are called cosignificators of the querent and the Moon is always a cosignificator of the querent no matter where she is in the chart. If the 1st house is unoccupied, we have two significators for the querent, namely the ruler of the 1st and the Moon. Although the Moon is regarded as rather less powerful than the Lord of the Ascendant, we ignore her at our peril for, on occasion, her influence is decisive!

But the Moon is a problem. It is not unknown for Cancer, the sign she rules, to be on the cusp of the house governing the question. Say we are asking a question about a partner—then we have to look at the 7th house. But if Cancer is on the cusp of 7, or if the Moon is in 7, the Moon is also the significator of the other party—the quesited. In a case like this, most horary practitioners are inclined to drop the Moon from her role as significator of the querent. Nevertheless, in some instances, the Moon still seems to provide information about the querent. The main reason for this is that she retains a very important function: without lunar aspects there is no progress in the matter under consideration and nothing happens (see the section on The Moon Void of Course in chapter 6). Therefore, it is essential to look at the Moon every time. Even though she may tell us about the other party, we also need her for the querent, and she is indispensable if we want to say anything about how the situation will develop.

Thus, on the strength of their rulerships, planets play an important part as significators of the querent and the quesited. But as soon as we start using the planets as house rulers, a new problem confronts us. Traditional horary astrology keeps to the classical rulers; which means that the trans-Saturnian planets, Uranus, Neptune and Pluto are left out of the reckoning. And so, Saturn—not Uranus—rules Aquarius, Mars—not Pluto—rules Scorpio, and Jupiter—not Neptune—rules Pisces. But some astrologers do use the trans-Saturnian planets as rulers, exactly as in character analysis. Therefore, one horary astrologer will use Mars as the ruler of Scorpio where another would use Pluto. Needless to say, this can produce differences in interpretation. After years of experimentation, I have found that both methods are clearly valid, and I should not want to forego using the classical rulers.

Barbara Watters suggested, quite plausibly, that a horary chart is a diagram of what the querent consciously or unconsciously knows at the moment he or she asks the question. Those things of which he or she is totally unaware at that moment, but which do in fact affect the result, must be present in the chart as mysterious or unpredictable factors. According to Watters, such factors are symbolized by the trans-Saturnian planets Uranus, Neptune, and Pluto; a good reason for putting the latter in a special category. In her opinion, we should stop using them as house rulers.

Her finding is that when the traditional planets give favorable answers but a trans-Saturnian planet points to difficulties, the idea that prompted the question is sound enough, but events beyond the querent's control will come in to spoil his or her chances. For example, previously unknown factors can emerge.

However, here she is talking about problems in which the trans-Saturnian planets can be interpreted as strange or unknown forces. If the question relates to some topic that is better represented by a trans-Saturnian planet than by one of the classical planets, the trans-Saturnian planet is the one to use (as Watters herself admits). A question about astrology, modern technology, aviation or the like, with Aquarius on the cusp of the house concerned, requires Uranus—not Saturn—as the significator of the quesited, because Saturn has much less affinity with things of this type.

Readers must decide for themselves which of the two to use—the classical or the trans-Saturnian rulers. If asked, I myself would say that, in principle, it is better to employ the classical rulers as significators, and then our judgment can be refined by an inspection of the trans-Saturnian rulers. But the trans-Saturnian rulers should be the main significators for things with which they have a special affinity.

C. *Decide which house or houses belong to the question.* It is extremely important to find the right house! If we are unable to reach a decision, help is available from *The Rulership Book* by Rex Bills—a veritable goldmine of astrological correspondences.[1] The quesited is symbolized by the ruler of the house concerned and by planets in that house. Suppose we have a question about the progress of our university studies, the ruler of 9 would be the significator and any planets in 9 would be cosignificators of the studies.

D. *Supplementary information is supplied by planets that have a natural relationship to the subject of the question.* Although the supplementary information is less important than that provided by the house to which the question belongs, the judgment is refined by this information and we obtain a better perspective of the course of events. If, for example, we have lost a ring, this is a valuable article and so comes under the 2nd house (and thus the ruler of 2 and planets in 2). But Venus is the natural ruler of valuables, and the placement of Venus in the chart can be very enlightening about this lost ring.

Not always will one planet be so applicable to the quesited. In that case, we can safely confine ourselves to the given house. Especially in complicated situations, where an object can be symbolized by several planets, it is sensible to stick to the houses.

E. *Renumber the houses if the question concerns a third party.* We must apply the rules given in chapter 4 if the question is not about ourselves or about the querent.

F. *Look at the traditional major aspects.* Many horary astrologers work exclusively with the conjunction (0°), the sextile (60°), the square (90°), the trine (120°), and the opposition (180°). The inconjunct (150°) is not generally used (or used only in a supplemental way). The parallel also plays an important role.

Aspects between the significators of the querent and the quesited are extremely important. If such aspects are absent and are not being formed, then there is literally no connection between the querent and the question, which is a negative indication. If the Moon also has no tie-in, the chart will not supply an answer. This rule has one or two small exceptions (see chapter 6) but they rarely occur.

---

[1] A new book has just been published entitled *The Book of Rulerships* by Dr. J. Lee Lehman (West Chester, PA: The Whitford Press, 1992). This book contains many unusual rulership possibilities collected from many of the older sources and may be of interest to students who want to explore horary to its fullest. Pub. note.

When there are many significators, there are likely to be many aspects. But with only one significator (plus the Moon, of course), there may well be no more than one aspect.

The orb of an aspect is important. The more exact the aspect, the quicker its effect. If there is an aspect with a wide orb, or a future aspect to come (so there is an even greater distance between the significators involved), then there might be something positive, but the way is increasingly open to alterations, complications and interventions. Sometimes the significators make no mutual aspects in the chart, but their aspects are getting ready to form. Although they are in prospect, the aspects are not yet within orb at the moment the question is asked. They offer hope on the question, but it is a rather uncertain hope, because various contingencies can block it.

In connection with the above, it is important to note applying aspects—aspects that are not yet exact. They inform us of the way things will develop. Separating aspects—or aspects which have already been exact—show what has already happened before the question was asked or before the event occurred. Separating aspects fill in the background, but they can not apprise us of the future. They have already done their work and have no further influence on anything. Therefore, we concentrate on the *applying major aspects*. The interpretation of the aspects is very much a black and white affair. In horary astrology, in contradistinction to natal astrology, we do call aspects "good" and "bad." The qualities of the aspects are as follows:

• *Conjunction:* joint action. It indicates that two people, or the querent and the querent's objective will come together. It is a positive aspect and brings to the querent the thing about which the inquiry has been made. Thus, a piece of lost property is returned, a wish is fulfilled, a marriage takes place, and so on.

• *Sextile:* this signifies opportunity; and one or more chances can present themselves for obtaining the desire. But, with a sextile, the querent always has to make an effort to get what is promised. It is not handed to him or her on a silver plater.

• *Trine:* the trine, too, represents chances and opportunities and, what is more, they are much easier to realize than with the sextile. It is a lucky aspect, and promises help and success without the querent having to do very much to attain it.

• *Square*: this is a tense aspect that warns of hindrances and difficulties. Considerable application and energy are needed in order to reach one's goal, *or* the goal is not reached, *or* it is reached at some cost, *or* when the goal is reached it does not come up to expectations, is not much benefit, *or* creates other problems.

• *Opposition*: another hard aspect. It points to separation. We do not get what we want. And if by hook or by crook we do reach our goal, it will be useless to us. Experience teaches that when the significator of the client or querent is involved in a number of oppositions, the querent does not take the astrologer's warnings seriously and refuses to believe the negative answer given by the chart. Therefore, the opposition is a difficult aspect—the querent flings good advice to the winds or acts foolishly, and the end result is disappointment.

• *The parallel*: this aspect is a little like the conjunction and generally brings the querent and the quesited together. Traditional horary specialists, in particular, are fond of the aspect; but it is not employed by all horary astrologers. On the basis of my own experience, I heartily recommend its use. Opinions differ, as to how it should be used. Some draw a distinction between the ordinary parallel and the split parallel or contraparallel. Others do not. I myself have found that *all* parallels have a positive uniting effect, but I have occasionally noticed in the case of the split parallel that the querent is seized with doubt or that something happens to cast doubt on the favorable course of events.

• *Inconjunct or Quincunx*: an aspect that is not often employed in ordinary horary astrology. However, according to some (and this agrees with my own experience), it does play a role in mundane charts and in charts of events. What is more, inconjuncts are connected with accidents, injuries, lost property, and so on. Therefore, astrologers who use this aspect strongly advise the querent not go on a journey if the event chart of the moment of departure contains several inconjunct aspects. In an event chart erected for the moment a journey starts, squares and oppositions warn of delays, but the inconjunct can spell danger.

G. *Confine the interpretation to the significators and to the houses concerned.* When we have identified the planets that represent the querent and the quesited, we must leave the rest of the chart out of consideration. However dramatic or splendid other aspects may be, they play absolutely no part in answering the question. This is a most important rule! The best procedure to adopt is to make a list of the relevant significators, together with the aspects they are about to form and their sign and house positions, without going on to look at the rest of the chart. It is very tempting to search for further indications; but there are really none to find, and any attempt to read meaning into other aspects and constellations will only confuse the issue. So we must keep to the matter in hand and leave well alone. All manner of errors flow from looking at the whole chart. In natal astrology this is something we do, but in horary astrology it is forbidden!

H. *Study the ephemeris to see if promising aspects between the significators will become perfect.* It sometimes happens that, just before a very promising aspect is perfect, one planet turns retrograde or the other passes into a different sign. Then the thing signified by the splendid aspect in the process of formation does not come to fruition. More will be said about this in the next chapter.

I. *Look at any major aspects the Moon has yet to make before she quits the sign.* Since the Moon is always the cosignificator of the querent, the applying aspects of the Moon, and any further aspects she makes, indicate future events connected with the matter or question being considered. If the next aspect and the last aspect are both favorable, the quesited should have a good beginning and a good end irrespective of what the intermediate aspects are like. The latter may spell trouble, but the final result will be good. The picture is quite different when the next aspect is easy and the last is difficult. Then the matter will begin well but end badly, or it will not come up to expectations, or nothing will come of it, and so on. Some disappointment may be expected when the last planet the Moon aspects is retrograde. A disappointment like this can be due to a change of mind of one of the parties, to a restriction from outside, to a mistake made by the querent when this retrograde planet is his or her significator, and so on. We also see that when the last aspect of the Moon is a square, the querent not only meets with difficulties, but has second thoughts or changes course. The parallel aspect must be included among the aspects studied.

　　If what should have been the Moon's last aspect in the series fails because the slower planet has meanwhile left the sign it was occupy-

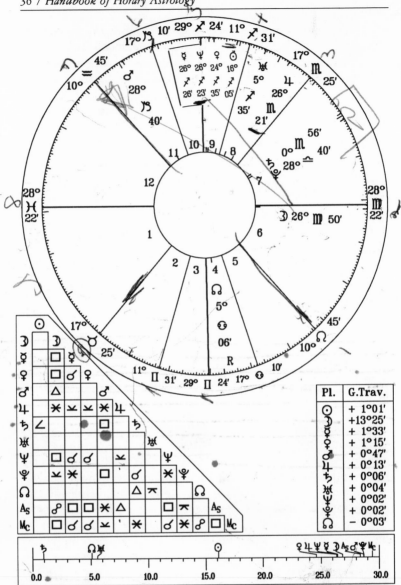

Chart 1. Event chart for opening a letter about dental care. Amsterdam, Holland (52 N 22, 4 E 54), December 8, 1982, 12:30 P.M. GMT. Placidus houses. Chart calculated by Astrolabe, using *Nova Printwheels*.

ing, then there is a strong possibility that the matter will be abruptly discontinued or that the querent will not get what he or she wants. Sometimes the querent just loses interest.

Examples

Chart 1 is an example of how the scope of a judgment can be restricted. The situation is as follows. When our first child was born we received a circular letter from the Dental Health Institute in Amsterdam, offering an opportunity for the child to receive twelve years' intensive dental care. The Dental Health Institute aimed to put people in touch with an affiliated dentist in their neighborhood, and I accordingly received a letter with the name and address of my new dental practitioner. The chart given here was erected for the moment I opened the letter. I was very surprised to see the restrictions on interpretation, especially as an Ascendant in the last degrees of a sign generally means that the inquiry is too late, the matter having already been decided. And yet, as far as I was concerned, I was making a fresh start with a new dentist. The time was noted very accurately; and with Pisces rising one needs to be careful, because the Ascendant passes through this sign very quickly, so that a small error in timing can make a big difference. The chart was properly erected.

Nevertheless, I did analyze the chart. My own indicators are Jupiter (and provisionally, Neptune) as ruler(s) of Pisces, Mars as ruler of the intercepted sign Aries, and of course the Moon. The Moon is in the 6th in the house of the dental practice. (A dentist falls under Mars and under Scorpio, but his practice is in the 6th house.) The significators of the dentist, if we use the 6th house, are the Sun as Lord of 6, and the Moon because she is posited in 6. Thus, the Moon represents both myself and the dentist, and so we may interpret the Moon in two senses.

As significator of myself, the Moon makes an applying trine to Mars. As already mentioned, a dentist is typified by Mars; and, in addition to the fact that the Moon is in 6, the applying harmonious aspect between the Moon and Mars is an indication that I shall go to this particular dentist. Yet Mars is also my own cosignificator—but more of this in a moment.

The Sun, which is the main significator of the dentist, stands in 9, and makes no immediate aspect with any of my significators, that is to say, with the Moon, Jupiter (Neptune) or Mars. To be sure, it will transit Neptune, but has to pass Venus first, and this prevents it from expressing itself properly.

So we have the following indications: a contact takes place, but it is not as positive as it might be, and there is something cut and dried about the situation, something that suggests that we are "too late" or will be frustrated by limitations in the interpretation.

I made an appointment with the dentist and received prompt attention. But when I was leaving, he said, "I wish you all the best. You have seen me for the first and last time. As from next month, this practice will be run by another dentist. I myself am going abroad." See the ruler of the 6th house — the Sun — in the 9th house of the horary chart! But note, too, that if we turn the chart for this dentist and treat the 6th house as the 1st, then the original 2nd house becomes the new 9th. This new 9th house was Venus as its ruler, and the first aspect made by the Sun is a conjunction with Venus, the ruler of the dentist's "foreign travel."

There is a rule which says that a new person or object always lies as many houses further on as the number of the old house in the chart. For example, say our house is 4, then the new house we are interested in will be the 4th from the 4th, and that is the 7th house in the chart. Applying this rule to the present case, we find that the new dentist is represented by the 6th house from the 6th, which is the 11th. In that house we find Mars as the significator of the new dentist, Saturn being the ruler of the house. Saturn is at 0°55′ Scorpio and has therefore just entered a new sign. When a planet is just inside a new sign, this usually means that whatever is indicated by the planet has also entered a new phase or new situation. The new dentist had only just taken over the practice.

The question was: should I go to this new dentist? And the answer was yes, because, as we have seen, the Moon makes a trine to Mars, the symbol of the new dentist. This is fortuitous but very appropriate, because Mars naturally represents dentists; and here, in the 6th from the 6th house, it points in a very remarkable way to the second dentist in this practice. What is more, Mars is one of my significators in this chart; which means my significator is actually in the house of the second dentist: another sign that I should go to him.

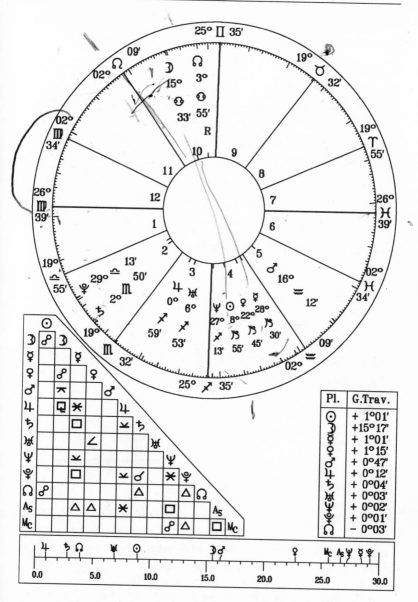

Chart 2. <u>Will I ever hear from her again?</u> Amsterdam, Holland (52 N 22, 4 E 54), December 30, 1982, 10:45 P.M. GMT. Placidus houses. Chart calculated by Astrolabe, using *Nova Printwheels*.

It is good to pause for a moment and take a look at the applying aspect between the Moon and Mars, because it is open to various interpretations:

• the Moon, as significator of dentist Number One (the Moon is in 6) is making a harmonious aspect with Mars, as significator of me (Mars is co-ruler of 1);

• the Moon, as significator of me, makes an applying trine to Mars as general significator of a dentist;

• the Moon, as significator of me, makes an applying trine to Mars as specific significator of the second dentist (Mars stands in the 6th from the 6th house).

Thus the same aspect brought about satisfactory (because a trine is involved) contacts with both dentists. This example shows that we can still do something with a horary chart when there are restrictions on interpretation, provided we do not jump to conclusions.

Now for another example. This time, we shall use one that illustrates the value of parallel aspects. An acquaintance told me a long story one evening about the difficulties she had been having with a girlhood friend over the past year, a friend with whom she had always got on well. Their differences had become so great that they had broken off their friendship. During her recital she suddenly asked, "What do you think, shall I ever hear from her again?"

In the horary chart for the moment the question was asked, the querent is symbolized by Mercury (Virgo Ascendant) and the Moon. (See Chart 2 on p. 39.) The Ascendant falls just outside the interpretation restrictions. Also, we notice that Cusp 12 and the Ascendant occupy the same sign. This suggests that the querent's problems were partly her own fault, which was true.

The Sun, as Lord of 11 (because Leo is on the cusp of the 11th house) represents the friend. There is no connection, or prospect of any connection, between the Sun and Mercury. The Moon has made a recent opposition with the Sun—an indication of the break between the two people concerned in the recent past. There are no other indications; so that, on these grounds, we should be forced to conclude that there is no immediate prospect of a reconciliation. However, on looking at future aspects of the Moon, we see, one after the other, an opposition to Venus, a parallel with the Sun, an inconjunct with

Neptune, a parallel with Venus, a square with Pluto and an opposition to Mercury.

The Moon is going to make a parallel with the Sun, which could re-establish communications, but first it makes an opposition to Venus, and this might tend to spoil things. Venus is ruler of Taurus, and Taurus is on cusp 9. The 9th house is the 11th house of the 11th house, and so represents the friends of the querent's girlhood friend and also tells us something about the attitude of the friend toward friendships generally. Therefore the opposition can give a contact, but it is not very promising. The parallel promises more, but the following aspect of the Moon (before she leaves the sign), gives little cause for optimism. Above all, the Moon in opposition to the querent's significator, Mercury, can be a sign that the querent will find it hard to cope with the situation. I came to the conclusion that some sort of renewed contact was possible, but that the querent should not expect too much from it.

A few days later a New Year's Greeting card arrived from the friend, whereupon the querent herself decided to telephone a day or two afterward. Although the exchange was amiable enough, the relationship was no longer what it was. And still the querent does not know how to handle the situation; her occasional contacts with her old friend seem to have very little left to offer.

6

More Rules of Interpretation

The last chapter dealt with a number of basic rules—rules that are of prime importance in analyzing the horary chart. But, in addition to the basic rules, there are many amplifications and refinements, which can sometimes completely alter the meaning of the chart. As we have seen, there is no universal agreement on such things as when not to judge a chart; and the same applies to the following niceties of interpretation. Where necessary, we shall discuss the different opinions and examine the practical value of these subsidiary rules.

Besiegement

Besiegement is when the last-formed aspect of the Moon was hard and with a so-called malefic, and the next aspect of the Moon will also be hard and made with a malefic. Traditionally, Mars and Saturn are "bad" planets and are also known as malefics. After the discovery of the trans-Saturnian planets, a certain group of astrologers included in the malefics Uranus and Pluto and, to a lesser extent, Neptune. In practice, there are no good and bad planets in astrological character reading: each planet has its own mode of reaction and represents a distinct part of the psyche. In horary astrology, on the other hand, the interpretation is very black and white, and concepts such as good and bad are perfectly relevant. It is in this light that besiegement must be considered.

The Moon is the form-giver that can get things moving. If her last aspect has been difficult, the querent has already been facing problems; and, if her very next aspect is difficult, too, then these problems are not yet over by any means. In a case of this sort, the querent is finding the whole situation problematical, and a besieged Moon only adds to the trouble. The hard aspects concerned are the conjunction, the square and the opposition.

Some horary astrologers have extended the rule to cover the significators of the querent or the quesited. If the significator is besieged, this is regarded as a bad sign. There is much to be said for this, because already formed and presently forming hard aspects indicate problems in the past and in the future. DeVore limits besiegement to the situation where a benefic (a good planet such as Venus or Jupiter) is found between two malefics, and is also within the orb of an aspect. Naturally, this greatly restricts the number of times besiegement can occur. Ivy Goldstein-Jacobson, on the other hand, maintains that when a significator is placed between two malefics, regardless of the number of signs between them and regardless of whether or not there are any aspects, then the significator is, so to speak, imprisoned by two evil forces. With her, Mars and Saturn are the main malefics. She adds that the besiegement is less serious when the malefics are further away from the significator.[1]

In my own practice, I have not had any convincing results with besiegement in the latter sense of the word. But I have certainly had some quite good results with besiegement in the first sense of the word (that is to say, with the Moon in the act of passing from one difficult aspect to another).

---

[1]The editor also wanted to mention that the old definition of besiegement is also discussed by Coley. On page 41 of *Clavis Astrologae*, he says that "a planet is said to be besieged when he is between the bodies of Saturn and Mars, so Jupiter in 10° of Gemini, Saturn in 4° and Mars in 14° here Jupiter is besieged of Saturn and Mars." In more modern terms, students might call this planetary containment.

Debility

The action of a planet is debilitated when it stands in a sign in which it can not really express its true nature. We also speak of a planet's debility when, even if it is fairly well placed by sign, it has a number of difficult aspects with so-called malefics, or is retrograde, has no assistance from benefics or is in similar adverse circumstances. Sometimes the situation where the significator is between two malefics is called a debility, but this is really a besiegement. In any case, there is little difference between the two situations.

To determine where a planet is well-placed and where badly placed, we must turn to the section on Exaltation and Fall (see p. 80).

The best way of looking at debility is to see it as a situation in which a planet, through position in sign, house, and/or aspect, has lost too much energy to hold its own, because its placement does not help it to make the most of itself. Obviously, when the Moon or a significator is affected in such a way, it can do little good for the question.

Critical and Other Degrees

In Hindu astrology, the zodiac is divided into twenty-eight sections, known as the Lunar Mansions. Each Lunar Mansion is 12° 51′ 25″ in size, or roughly 13°. On dividing the zodiac from 0° Aries in this manner, we find the starting points shown in Table 2. These starting

Table 2. Lunar Mansions or Critical Degrees.

Signs	Degrees	Nearest degree in round numbers
Cardinal signs	0° 00′ 00″	0°
	12° 51′ 25″	13°
	25° 42′ 50″	26°
Fixed signs	8° 34′ 15″	9°
	21° 25′ 40″	21°
Mutable signs	4° 17′ 05″	4°
	17° 08′ 30″	17°

points of the Hindu Lunar Mansions have been borrowed by Western astrology because of their importance, and are known to us as critical degrees. We use the values rounded to the nearest degree, and this gives us the following critical degrees:

Aries, Cancer, Libra, Capricorn: 0°, 13° and 26°
Taurus, Leo, Scorpio, Aquarius: 9° and 21°
Gemini, Virgo, Sagittarius, Pisces: 4° and 17°.

The meaning of the critical degrees is—crisis! When the Moon, or the significator of the querent or the quesited, stands in a critical degree, the matter has reached a critical point or has been driven to extremes; a crisis will arise, an illness will follow, or there is a danger of quarrels or disagreements and the like.

One or two other degrees are important, too. If the Moon or a significator is at 0°, that is to say, in the first degree of *any* sign, we have to take into consideration that it has entered a new sign. This means that fresh developments have recently taken place regarding the question and that they are going to develop further. The Moon or the significator has entered a new situation.

If a planet is in 29° of a sign, that is to say, in the last degree, then changes—even big changes—are about to take place. The last degree of a sign is often regarded as rather unfavorable or full of problems; but, although this may be partly true, a great deal depends on the change of sign itself and on the nature of the planet concerned. If the Moon is 0° Taurus, she has just left Aries, where she is much less at home than she is in Taurus. This recent change is beneficial to the querent; therefore, its further development is likely to be beneficial, too. Mars in 29° Libra is in a sign in which it is not free to deploy its resources as significator of the querent, the quesited, or some object (see Exaltation and Fall, p. 80). Nevertheless, it is on the point of entering Scorpio, of which it is co-ruler with Pluto. The change about to occur will be positive for the querent. If Mars is in the last degree of Virgo, and therefore about to enter Libra, the change will be much less favorable.

Similar considerations apply to a planet at 15° of a sign, i.e., right in the middle of the sign. This position suggests a settled and peaceful course of events, and that matters are stable. However, we need to be wary where the fixed signs are concerned, because this 15° position sometimes indicates the risk of a stalemate.

If we pay attention to the derivation of the critical degrees, we see for example that the ninth degree in fixed signs is really a rounding off from 8° 34′ 15″. Some astrologers, especially those who use degree symbolism, take the ninth degree from 8° 01′ through 9° 59′ as a critical degree. Others consider 9° 00′ through 9° 59′ to be the ninth, and critical, degree. This means that different schools of thought treat different degrees as critical; however, the majority regard the latter possibility, that is to say, from 9° 00′ through 9° 59′ as correct. In a case like this, where the starting point is almost halfway between two degrees (8° 34′ 15″), I look at both possibilities, although I prefer the latter.

Decanates

The zodiac signs are 30° each. Each sign has its own ruler; some signs even have two. In this case, the day dispositor or ruler is more important than the night dispositor or ruler (see chapter 1).

As we have already discussed, the classical rulers are given preference in horary astrology, although Uranus, Neptune and Pluto must not be ignored.

Each sign can be further divided into decanates. Each decanate spans an arc of 10°, and so each sign contains three decanates. The sign ruler is Lord of its decanate, but these also have their own rulers. There are two methods in use for determining the Lords of the decanates or faces:

• A method based on the sequence of the signs within a single element;

• The Chaldean method.

The first variant is what is most used in character analysis, where the Chaldean method is practically unknown. The determination of the decanate rulers based on the elements goes as follows:

• The first decanate, that is to say, the first 10° of a sign, merely has as ruler the main ruler of the sign in question. For example, the first 10° of Aries is ruled by Mars, the first 10° of Taurus by Venus, and so on.

• the second decanate is ruled by the day dispositor of the following sign in the same element. Thus the second 10° of Aries is ruled by the Sun, because Leo is the next fire sign after Aries. Nevertheless, the natural Lord of Aries—Mars—remains co-ruler of the decanate.

• the third decanate of Aries is ruled by the day dispositor of the third sign in the same element; that is to say it is ruled by Jupiter, the Lord of Sagittarius. Again, Mars is co-ruler.

Turning now to earth sign Capricorn, we find Saturn ruling the first decanate. Over the second decanate rule Saturn and Venus, the ruler of Taurus. Over the third decanate rule Saturn and Mercury, the Lord of Virgo. Thus we take the sign we are dividing as the first sign of that element.

In certain cases, the decanates have a value in interpretation. If a significator or the Moon occupies a decanate it rules, its power is increased and it exerts more influence. But, if it is not well-placed in this respect, then the scope of its influence is reduced; and this is even more certain if it is also involved in difficult aspects. For instance, the Moon is not well-placed in Scorpio. However, the Moon does rule over the last decanate of Scorpio. In that position, the Moon certainly makes its presence felt, but not in a particularly positive way.

The second variant, the Chaldean, works as follows. The zodiac is divided into the same 36 decanates, and Mars rules the first decanate of the zodiac, which runs from 0° through 10° Aries. The sequence of the decanate rulers then follows this pattern: Mars, Sun, Venus, Mercury, Moon, Saturn, Jupiter. The pattern keeps on repeating itself. This means that the second decanate of Aries, from 10° through 20°, is ruled by the Sun, and the third, from 20° through 30°, is ruled by Venus. In the third decanate, we start to diverge from the rulerships according to the elements. The entire series is shown in Table 3. The trans-Saturnian planets—Uranus, Neptune and Pluto—are absent. The cycle begins and ends with the planet Mars. Although this allocation of the rulers is little used, there are a few horary specialists who speak very highly of it.

When interpreting a chart using both the basic rules and the refinements given in the present chapter, we shall often find that we do not need the decanates, because the rest of the chart already speaks for itself. But sometimes we may be in doubt, and then the decanates and their rulers can be brought in as supportive evidence on one side or another; and it will be found that the two methods, although they

Table 3. Chaldean Rulerships.

Sign	First Decanate	Second Decanate	Third Decanate
Aries	Mars	Sun	Venus
Taurus	Mercury	Moon	Saturn
Gemini	Jupiter	Mars	Sun
Cancer	Venus	Mercury	Moon
Leo	Saturn	Jupiter	Mars
Virgo	Sun	Venus	Mercury
Libra	Moon	Saturn	Jupiter
Scorpio	Mars	Sun	Venus
Sagittarius	Mercury	Moon	Saturn
Capricorn	Jupiter	Mars	Sun
Aquarius	Venus	Mercury	Moon
Pisces	Saturn	Jupiter	Mars

may seem to conflict with one another, are both useful in practice. Without doubt, the reader will develop a preference for one of the methods, and this will then be the one that gives the best results.

The North and South Nodes

The North and South Nodes are not heavenly bodies but astronomical points of intersection in the heavens. We all know that, as seen from Earth, the planets and the Sun and Moon seem to move more or less in the plane of the ecliptic. The ecliptic is, for us on Earth, the projection of the *apparent* annual path of the Sun around Earth as seen against the background of the zodiac. The planes of the planetary orbits diverge very little from the plane of the ecliptic. The plane of the Moon's orbit is inclined to the plane of the ecliptic at an angle of 5° 17'. Therefore, in her path around Earth, the Moon cuts the plane of the ecliptic twice: once on her way up; this point of intersection is called the Moon's North (or Ascending) Node, or the Dragon's Head—and once on her way down; and this point is called the Moon's South (or Descending) Node, or the Dragon's Tail. The symbols are respectively ☊ and ☋. The North Node and the South Node are diametrically opposite one another in the Zodiac. Since the Lunar nodes are simply points in the heavens and not heavenly bodies, we must not interpret them as planets, or as psychic factors. Their meanings can be derived as follows:

What we are dealing with is points of intersection of the orbital planes of the two Lights—the Sun and Moon. Symbolically, when the two planes coincide, there is a union of the conscious (Sun) and the unconscious (Moon). But what does this union mean? The Sun and Moon not only symbolize conscious and unconscious, they also symbolize Yang and Yin, day and night, male and female, etc. In the astrology of relationships, the North and South nodal axis is endowed with a very important role by this male/female union, because in concrete terms this refers to the union of man and wife. And, in fact, this gives a sort of union between conscious and unconscious, as Jungian psychology indicates. Our task in life is to integrate the conscious and the unconscious. We come to know the contents of our own unconscious from our intimate relationships, especially from the relationship with a life partner. Unconscious factors are projected from ourselves onto the other person, and we can learn to handle them through our intimate relationship with that person.

The lunar nodes seem to be important in partnerships and deep friendships. Relationships bring us continually nearer to ourselves and to our destiny. Obviously, this is not always easy. It means noticing things about ourselves that we would rather not see; it means seeing and coming to terms with faults, character defects, repressions that stand in the way of our development, and so on. Thus, although it has to do with self-fulfillment, the North and South nodal axis is certainly not the easiest axis in the chart—far from it! Perhaps that is why Hindu astrology regards the North Node as something disagreeable and fatal, although this is a very black and white view.

Horary astrology does, however, share the Hindu concept that fate is somehow involved in the North and South Nodes. Planets, or points such as the Ascendant or Midheaven, receive extra emphasis when they are in the same degree as the North Node, regardless of what sign they are in, and their importance for interpretation is increased. Thus, if the North Node is 3° 14' Cancer and Saturn is 3° 55' Scorpio, then Saturn is in the same degree as the North Node. The fact that it is also making a trine to the North Node is neither here nor there, because we do not work with aspects to the North Node in horary astrology. It is simply because Saturn is in the same *degree* as the North Node (irrespective of sign) that the planet gains an emphasis which sometimes must be treated as negative, but in any case, difficult. A danger lurks, a troublesome situation threatens to arise, and so on. This emerges even more strongly when Saturn is a significator of the querent or the quesited.[2]

Nevertheless, the emphasis is not always completely negative. If the chart in general is favorable, then a beneficial planet in the same degree as the North Node (again irrespective of sign) may indicate that fate is going to play into our hands, especially if the aspects to this planet are harmonious. Events of a worrying or tragic nature can work out in our favor in a way we would never have expected. Thus we can suddenly be given a brilliant promotion due to the death of our boss. Or our own business can suddenly make a big profit owing to the mistake of a competitor, or we can cash in when foreign competitors are hit by strikes, etc. The situation or event is completely beyond our control; but, by a twist of fate, we manage to do well out of it. The "difficulty" as far as we are concerned, could be in making up our minds to act when the opportunity comes our way and in working out the best method of doing so.

Therefore, in horary astrology, the North Node/South Node[3] axis expresses what fate secretly has in store and we cannot prevent. But this is still not the full meaning. If, for instance, we have a query about some relationship, the Dragon's Head will very often provide supplementary information about it, wholly in the light of the above. We are confronted with a number of things that we are no longer able to avoid; we have to come to terms with them, either by taking the relationship further or by putting it right. It is as if we were receiving instructions to look at the problem honestly and to do something about it. If we try to suppress the problem again, the same sort of situation will recur with the North and South Nodes once more confronting us with what we do not wish to see.

The North and South Nodes differ in character. The North Node (which is the one invariably given in ephemerides) is Jupiter-like, and the South Node, which is always in the same degree and minute but in the opposite sign, is Saturn-like. We take this into consideration when studying their house placements.

---

[2]For an example of a planet in the same degree as the North Node, see Chart 3 on page 70.

[3]Students who find this idea interesting should see Barbara Watters' book, *Horary Astrology and the Judgment of Events* (Washington, DC: Vashama, 1973) p. 96.

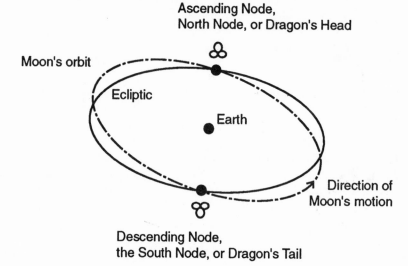

Figure 5. The relationship of the North and South Node to the Moon and Earth.

However that may be, we ought to pay extra attention to planets or points occupying exactly the same degree as the North Node. A warning, an unexpected development, or a learning process are often involved.

Nowadays, we have a special problem with the North and South Nodes. We used to work in astrology with the average position of the North Node; that is to say, we did not note the true position of the point of intersection (which is subject to small fluctuations) but with its mean position. This mean position is always what is given in the older ephemerides. Today, however, more and more people are in favor of taking the true position, and in a few modern ephemerides we find this listed, sometimes along with the mean position and sometimes without. Because the true position sometimes takes us into a different degree of the zodiac, the choice can be important in interpretation. In horary astrology, however, one always works with the mean position of the North Node and this proves to be very satisfactory. It is therefore absolutely safe to keep to the mean North Node although there can be no harm in experimenting with the true position.

Eclipses

In astrology we use two kinds of eclipse—the eclipse of the Sun and the eclipse of the Moon. The eclipse can be partial, in which only a part of the Sun or Moon is covered, or total, in which they are no longer visible.

In an eclipse of the Sun, the Moon intrudes itself between Earth and the Sun, so that some or all of the latter cannot be seen from the Earth. This means that an eclipse of the Sun is possible only at the New Moon, i.e., at the conjunction of the Sun and Moon. Nevertheless, by no means does every New Moon bring an eclipse of the Sun.

In an eclipse of the Moon, Earth passes exactly between the Sun and the Moon and cuts off the light to the Moon. In other words, the Moon is lying inside the cone of shadow cast by Earth. So an eclipse of the Moon can take place only at Full Moon, when the Sun and Moon are in opposition. But here, too, not every Full Moon brings an eclipse of the Moon.

In fact, a number of conditions have to be satisfied before we can speak of an eclipse. As we have already seen in the section on the North and South Nodes, the orbital planes of the Sun and Moon are inclined to one another at a small angle. If the conjunction (New Moon) or opposition (Full Moon) occurs when the Moon is too far from the North and South Nodes, there is no possibility of an eclipse because the two heavenly bodies are not in the same plane. The nearer the conjunction or opposition takes place to the North and South nodal axis (that is to say, the nearer the Sun and Moon are to being in the same plane), the greater the chance of a partial eclipse. If the orbital planes approach each other very closely indeed during a conjunction or opposition or, of course, if they coincide, the eclipse will be total.

In many ephemerides, the day and often the Greenwich time of the eclipse is given. This is important, not only for political astrology (in which eclipses are always full of portent), but also for horary astrology, where eclipses have special meaning. If a question is asked on the day of an eclipse of the Sun, the subject of this question will undergo one or more very far-reaching changes, or the whole matter fails. Anyway, it is impossible for things to stay as they are, because an eclipse of the Sun upsets everything.

Because the Sun and Moon have orbits which gradually approach one another and gradually separate, eclipses of the Moon occur about fourteen days before or after eclipses of the Sun. Earlier or later than this, the North and South nodal axis is too far away. Now when there is an eclipse of the Moon following an eclipse of the Sun, the above-mentioned radical change promised by the solar eclipse is introduced, or can be introduced, by the lunar eclipse. We say "can" advisedly, because it is sometimes possible to save the situation, even if only in a modified form. But then, at the time of the lunar eclipse, one has to keep a careful check on what is going on; otherwise there will be problems.

The house in which the eclipse falls must also be considered, of course, because the matters represented by that house are usually turned upside down or suffer considerable alteration. If the house has something to do with the question, then there is an even greater need for us to make some big changes on our own account, otherwise we shall have to face a crisis.

If, in addition, the eclipse falls on a so-called malefic, and especially on Mars or Saturn, the darkness and obscurity is intensified. The question may involve hidden or unexplained difficulties, or dishonesty or danger, and so on. By analogy with the unusual dimming of the two Lights,[4] we find that when the house in which the eclipse falls symbolizes a certain person connected with the question, then that person may need (stronger) glasses. And, because the Moon is co-significator of the querent, he or she may also need to consult an optician. But the conjunction of an eclipse and a malefic provides no information as to the gravity of the condition.

Mars takes approximately two years to complete a circuit of the zodiac and, in these two years, it comes once into conjunction with the eclipse point, twice into square aspect, and once into opposition. This provides the querent with critical data on the question, because Mars can have a very negative effect in such positions—often bringing matters to an untimely end, especially when the situation has not been kept under review.

A sudden eruption, either political or geological, can also be heralded by an eclipse of the Sun, which may be associated with coups d'état, assassinations, riots and warfare, not to mention earthquakes and other natural disasters. There is an increased danger of traffic,

---

[4] The Sun and the Moon.

aviation, or railway accidents, especially in countries where the eclipse was visible. But we need the charts of these countries in order to calculate the precise effects of the solar eclipse (among other things, by referring to the house in which the eclipse falls, to any planets aspected by the eclipse, etc.).

There is another form of eclipse, known as an occultation. Generally speaking, no notice is taken of this in interpretation unless additional information is required, and then it will be found to signify something unfavorable. We speak of an occultation when the Moon is conjunct a planet with the same declination. In this position, the planet is no longer visible from the Earth because the Moon obscures it.

While we are on the subject of eclipses, it might be well to add that if a New Moon (Sun conjunct Moon) without an eclipse is in houses 2, 3, 4, or 5, and the querent's ruler is also in one of these houses, matters will be rather obscure. Everything lies below the horizon in the night region of the chart, and the question is likely to be unclear, badly expressed, or prompted by hidden motives. In short, we need to be on our guard against getting on the wrong track in interpretation. Often, before the chart is studied and explained, it is a great help to have another talk with the querent to clarify the question. Some astrologers reckon an even greater area of obscurity, namely from half of the 1st house to halfway through the 6th house.

Translation of Light

When the significators of the querent and the quesited are linked by a separating aspect, that is to say an aspect that has already been exact, this means that the contact has already taken place. But that is very unhelpful for the development of the situation, because there is no new aspect or connection between the querent and the quesited coming along. However, there is one way in which a contact can still occur, and that is when a third and swifter planet aspects first one significator and then the other. We then say that the third planet translates light from one to the other. Very often this third planet represents a third party who gives voluntary help, or it may represent favorable circumstances. In order to decide precisely what it means, we must look at its nature and at the house over which it rules. It is important to note that this third planet must aspect the two significators one after the other; but, in the meantime, it also must not form an aspect to some other planet. If it does, we have a situation in which the fourth planet can interpose its own influence, and this is a negative development as far as the question is concerned.

Some astrologers restrict translation of light to the Moon. This is not so strange, because, among other things, the Moon is always the fastest moving, and we must always have a planet that is quicker than the two significators. However, it is always possible for some other planet to be moving faster than the two significators, especially when a normally swift significator (such as Mercury or Venus) is almost stationary in the zodiac around the time when it is turning retrograde or direct. At such time, Jupiter, for example, can move faster than Mercury or Venus, and thus fulfill the role of the third party.

Sometimes we encounter variations on the translation of light theme; but, in every case, two features have to be present — no further aspect must be formed between the two significators, and the third planet must link the two rulers by aspecting them one after the other. That is to say, we do not find translation of light so often in its pure form (which does not crop up very often), but variants are common enough.

The Part of Fortune and other Arabian Points

The Part of Fortune, or *Pars Fortunae*, is one of the so-called sensitive points that were in vogue among the Arabs in the Middle Ages. The Arabian Points are certainly not mathematical tricks based on whims, as some people think, but are based on the solar or sun houses. If the degree occupied by the Sun is used as the Ascendant (as is done in a flat chart when the time of birth is unknown), twelve equal, thirty-degree houses can be formed starting from that point. Say the Sun is 13° 24′ Gemini, and this is treated as the Ascendant. The 2nd house would begin at 13° 24′ Cancer, the 3rd at 13° 24′ Leo, and so on. When such a chart is erected, the position of the Moon in this new horoscope coincides with the position of the Part of Fortune in the original geocentric house system. This means that the Part of Fortune in the original horoscope lies as far from the original Ascendant as the Moon in the solar chart (with the Sun on the Ascendant) lies from the Sun.

In the same way, Mercury determines the Point of Trade and Intercourse, Venus the Point of Love, and so on. To avoid having to turn the chart, in order to use the Sun's position as the substitute Ascendant, the Arabs devised formulae for calculating the positions of these sensitive points on the basis of the true moment of birth.

Refinements were soon introduced, and a large number of new sensitive points following the same system were proposed. It goes without saying, that once you admit a series of sensitive points based on making the position of the Sun the Ascendant, you can go on to make another series with the Moon as starting point, or with Mercury or Venus, etc. One can also take the house cusps as new Ascendants — even that has happened.

The formulae are simple. The Part of Fortune, for example, can be found by adding the longitude of the Ascendant to the longitude of the Moon and subtracting the longitude of the Sun from the result. In brief:

The Part of Fortune = Ascendant + Moon – Sun.

Say the Ascendant is 16° 31′ Cancer, the Moon 21° 38′ Leo, and the Sun 15° 08′ Aquarius. First we convert these positions into degrees counted from 0° Aries, and arrive at the following:

Ascendant 16° 31′ Cancer (3 × 30° + 16° 31′) = 106° 31′
Moon 21° 38′ Leo (4 × 30° + 21° 38′) = 141° 38′
Sun 15° 08′ Aquarius (10 × 30° + 15° 08′) = 315° 08′

Now comes the calculation:

$$\begin{array}{r} 106° \ 31′ \\ + \ 141° \ 38′ \\ \hline 248° \ 09′ \end{array}$$

It is impossible to subtract the longitude of the Sun from this, so we add another 360°.

$$+ \underline{360° \ 00'}$$
$$608° \ 09'$$
$$\underline{-315° \ 08'}$$
$$293° \ 01' \quad \text{or } 23° \ 01' \text{ Capricorn } (9 \times 30° + 23° \ 01').$$

Controversy still rages over the value of the Part of Fortune and the other Arabian Points. Opinions are very divided. We find as many fierce opponents as staunch advocates of these points, and the reader will have to try them and decide whether he or she can work with them or not. Many of the points have fallen into oblivion, but the Part of Fortune has survived. In horary astrology it is still very much used, although not by all horary specialists.

W.J. Simmonite informs us that the Part of Fortune in a horary chart is less significant than the North and South Nodes, but that we must take its place into consideration in questions about money, lotteries, accounts and the like.[5] He adds that the Part of Fortune can cast the deciding vote when the factors for and against are evenly balanced.

A renowned horary specialist who used the Arabian Points a great deal is Ivy M. Goldstein-Jacobson.[6] In her experience, the Part of Fortune in a horary chart has a decidedly positive, ameliorating effect; it means "substance." If the Part of Fortune receives a favorable aspect from the Moon, the matter is strongly improved. Even if the Moon makes no aspect except a parallel to the Part of Fortune, the parallel aspect will save the Moon from being void of course.[7] The Part of Fortune brings both mental and material riches according to the condition of the querent's significator.[8] I also heard from one of her students that Goldstein-Jacobson also considered that the Part of Fortune in an Angle is a favorable sign. It is unfortunate only in the 8th or 12th house, and even then it may not be unfortunate unless it is afflicted or conjunct an adverse fixed star. She also says that it is a bad

---

[5]W. J. Simmonite, *Horary Astrology: The Key to Astrological Prediction* (Tempe, AZ: American Federation of Astrologers, 1950).

[6]Ivy M. Goldstein-Jacobson, *Simplified Horary Astrology with Requisite Mathematics* (Alhambra, CA: Frank Severy Publications, 1975).

[7]For those students not familiar with the Void of Course Moon, Lilly (loc. cit.) defines it this way: "A Planet is void of course, when he is separated from a Planet, nor doth forthwith, during his being in that Sign, apply to any other." Trans. note.

[8]Ivy M. Goldstein-Jacobson, *Simplified Horary Astrology with Requisite Mathematics*, pp. 97, 116.

omen when the Part of Fortune is in Pisces or Scorpio or in a Pisces or Scorpio decanate, or is in conflicting aspect with Mars or with Neptune. Nor is it particularly good if the Part of Fortune is in the same degree as the North Node, or in 29° of a sign. Goldstein-Jacobson and a number of European astrologers use the following points:

> Sickness: ASC + Mars – Saturn
> Marriage: ASC + DSC – Venus
> Solemnization of Marriage: Cusp 9 + Cusp 3 – Venus
> Surgery: ASC + Saturn – Mars
> Death: ASC + Cusp 8 – Moon
> Peril: ASC + Ruler of 8 – Saturn
> Legalization: Cusp 9 + Cusp 3 – Venus

The formula ASC + Mercury – Moon is applied to friends, confidence, shyness, timidity, travel and to all sorts of things! As refinements, there are other formulae for different kinds of travel such as:

> Travel Over Land: ASC + Cusp 9 – Ruler of 9
> Travel Over Sea: ASC + 16° Cancer – Saturn

My own experience with these points is such that I do not miss them when they are left out of account. The horary chart provides enough information without these points. This is not to say that they are not used with success by some horary specialists. All I can do is to advise readers to study the Arabian Points to determine their usefulness.

Reception

Reception (sometimes termed mutual reception) occurs when two planets occupy one another's signs. Say, for example, that Jupiter is in Cancer and the Moon in Sagittarius; then Jupiter is in the sign ruled by the Moon and the Moon is in the sign ruled by Jupiter. When two planets are in reception, the effect can be compared to that of a conjunction. Although, in psychological astrology, a reception must not be interpreted in quite the same way as a conjunction, in horary astrology it may certainly be considered as a normal conjunction. Except for one or two minor exceptions, a reception is always supportive and helpful. If one of the planets is insufficient in some respect, the other springs to its aid—or nearly always. However, if the second planet is also in difficulties, so to speak, the aid it can offer may be of little value.

In a reception, we have to proceed as follows. Let us suppose that, in the above example, the Moon is posited at 19° Sagittarius, and Jupiter at 12° Cancer. We then say that Jupiter is in the place of the Moon; and, since it is considered to be in conjunction with the Moon, we frame our interpretation as if Jupiter were at 19° Sagittarius, the degree occupied by the Moon. Similarly, the Moon is treated as if it were at 12° Cancer, the degree occupied by Jupiter. All aspects of the Moon are regarded as also being made to Jupiter, and all aspects to Jupiter as also being made to the Moon.

If a planet is weak by position or aspect, it gains strength from its reception partner; for instance, by treating it as being at the place of (= conjunct) its reception partner, we immediately find that it is in a better position and that it benefits from better aspects.

Of course, a reception is more important for a question if one of the significators of the querent or of the quesited is involved in that reception. The significator can gain great advantage from the intervention of its reception partner. The latter then represents a helpful third party. Quite often, this third-party planet supplies an escape route. If, for example, we are liable to pay a fine, the reception partner indicates some form of assistance that enables us to escape paying the fine or to have it forgiven. Or, suppose we are saddled with an uncongenial business partnership, the person represented by the reception planet is someone who can help us dissolve the partnership without too much trouble. In other words, a reception often shows some way out of a difficulty, such as an escape clause or the like.

The reader should take note that the traditional rulers of signs are the ones employed in receptions; thus Saturn (not Uranus only) is used for Aquarius, Mars (not Pluto only) for Scorpio, and Jupiter (not Neptune only) for Pisces. This increases the number of possible receptions. But, in the practice of horary astrology, it has been found to produce results. Thus, if the Moon is in Pisces and Jupiter in Cancer, we speak of a reception.

A reception with a significator that is important to the question can indicate that a certain problem can be overcome with the help of the reception partner. But, if the reception partner itself is in a very difficult position in the chart, the opposite can turn out to be true; so that we can run into more difficulties than the rest of the chart would lead us to expect.

It regularly happens that the significators of two parties (for example, in questions concerning the sale or purchase of a house, the significators of seller and buyer) are in mutual reception. The reception carries considerable weight when we come to assess the significance of any aspect between the two planets:

• When two significators make a square or an opposition and are also in reception, then there are certainly (many) problems to solve before the goal can be reached, but help is at hand for facing these problems, so that the outcome can be more positive than appears at first sight;

• When the reception partners are sextile or trine to one another, or make a parallel aspect, then both parties will very quickly reach a decision or make an agreement that is advantageous to them both;

• Sometimes, in the dissolution of a partnership (for example, in a divorce), a reception between the two significators, if they are in opposition, can point to a harmonious dividing of the assets. There is a goodwill over the division of the property, and this goodwill emanates from each partner;

• When there is no aspect, or only minor aspects are present, then the reception offers the chance to alter course before the paths separate, so the two partners can pursue their own interests without interfering with one another. And this can prove to be profitable for them both.

Even now, we have not exhausted the subject of receptions. If the significator of the querent is in reception, he or she should find it useful or advantageous to develop activities in the house occupied by the reception partner. Something of that sort can work out extremely well when the house itself is involved in the question. For the significator of the querent itself comes, so to speak, right into that house via the reception. When this is the case, it is often an indication that the querent can use his or her power, insight, and will to guide the course of the question; he or she has a certain amount of grip on the situation. But if the querent's significator is retrograde, then either the querent does not know what to do about the question, or he or she wishes to withdraw from it but is committed to it by the reception. Or he or she has no desire to enter the terrain of the reception partner. Fear or unwillingness are sometimes indicated by a retrograde significator in a reception. Anyway, receptions should never be ignored, for they generally offer ways out of trouble, as well as the means to achieve a positive result.

Retrograde Planets

The planetary positions used in horary astrology are those seen from Earth. They are called *geo*centric. If we were to record the positions of the planets in the zodiac as seen from the center of the solar system, that is to say from the Sun, they would be called *helio*centric. The Earth is not the center of the solar system, and the other planets do not travel in orbits around it. Therefore, we observe what appear to be irregularities in their paths. In reality, the planets, including Earth, always move in a direct motion around the Sun. But, as seen from Earth, it can look as if a planet is sometimes stationary, or sometimes even seems to move backward in the zodiac, that is to say, in the opposite direction to the one proper to it. Naturally, it is not really going backward, the whole thing is simply an optical illusion caused by the fact that we are looking at planets orbiting the Sun at different speeds from our own orbiting Earth. But this optical illusion is important both to astronomy (which calculates the positions of the heavenly bodies) and to the astrologer (who interprets their positions). We call this apparent backward course a retrograde motion.

There is less power and potential in a retrograde planet than in a direct planet. Therefore in horary astrology, retrograde motion is generally regarded as detrimental. However there are exceptions governed by the very symbolism implied in retrograde motion. By analogy, the fact that a planet is moving backward in the zodiac suggests that conditions are favorable for a return to an old situation. It is a fine indication for a reunion—since what is this but the restoration of an old situation? In questions about missing persons, animals, or things, it is always an advantage for their significators to be retrograde, as this is a sign of their return to their previous place. In questions about pending divorce, the Lord of 1 or the Lord of 7 retrograde suggests that one of the two parties will attempt a reconciliation, that is to say a return to the former situation. And the attempt will have a good chance of success if the two significators do not have too many conflicting aspects in the chart.

But the person who is involved in a love affair with someone, is likely to discover that the latter is already married or otherwise "spoken for." This person may feel pulled this way and that or may feel very unsure if the Lord of 7 is retrograde in the horary chart. In this instance a return to the old is definitely not good for the new (meaning possible marriage). In short, a retrograde planet puts a brake on anything new and renewing, while favoring a return to the old.

However, there are more possible interpretations. When the significator of a certain person is retrograde, this may mean that he or she is in a weak position, either in business matters or in health. Say we wish to make a purchase and the significator of the seller is retrograde; the latter will find himself or herself at a disadvantage. Experience teaches that the person indicated by a retrograde planet usually has second thoughts and withdraws.

Little action is initiated by a retrograde planet; often it represents the passive party. An individual who is indicated by a retrograde planet is more likely to become the victim of circumstances than is the individual with the direct significator. The "retrograde person" always shows little or no initiative whatever the circumstances, and usually beats a hasty retreat.

The retrograde motion of a planet can also indicate the withholding or suppression of information, if the planet is the significator of the quesited. Let us suppose we want to purchase a house and that the significator of the house — the ruler of 4 — is retrograde; this may mean that we are not being told everything about the state of the house; or, that as prospective purchasers we have not had a proper valuation or noticed the hidden defects. And if the house is purchased, the retrograde significator often shows that it will fail to come up to expectations. The result is generally a quick resale. Thus, there is something unsatisfactory about the information (not always through deliberate deception: sometimes the negligence of the purchaser is to blame), the property does not answer expectations and the purchaser will not keep it for very long. Nevertheless, there is one favorable, though rather infrequent, exception: this is when a purchaser wants to buy back a former possession. Then a retrograde significator comes into its own!

Often it turns out that the person symbolized by a retrograde planet was either ill or else feeling sick about something. This, too, is in keeping with the idea of weakness and concealment. And, on the subject of concealment, it is worth adding that, if the querent is indicated by a retrograde planet, there is a likelihood that he or she has not been completely frank, or does not care to reveal the full extent of the difficulties.

If you are intending to start something new, and the significator of the matter is retrograde, be on your guard; double check all plans and estimates. Often you will find that you have been over-optimistic, or that errors have crept in. Quite frequently, a transaction or project that started out with a retrograde significator becomes costly and full of problems. Return to the old; wait a while before beginning something new—this is the message of a retrograde significator.

A retrograde planet as significator of the querent, the quesited, or of some related issue shows a reluctance to set out on a fresh path. The person concerned prefers to see which way the cat jumps, and will not get involved. But if the retrograde planet is in a fixed sign (Taurus, Leo, Scorpio or Aquarius) then the new direction will have to be taken sooner or later.

If the question concerns a particular object, then a retrograde significator can mean that the object is not where it belongs. If it is in fact in its place, then it is in bad condition, the payment on it is in arrears or something of the sort.

Sometimes a retrograde planet can mean something for the question in its quality as a planet (not just as a house ruler). We need to watch out for this. It is especially true of the classical planets (Mercury, Venus, Mars, Jupiter and Saturn). When the trans-Saturnian planets are retrograde, there is a danger of subtle subversion. Often, what is subverted—or what will be subverted—is revealed only when the planet concerned turns direct. However, we must be careful how we apply this rule, because the three trans-Saturnian planets can remain retrograde for a very long time, and we can not possibly assume that for the greater part of a year we shall have to deal with all kinds of deceit and subtle undermining. An interpretation in this style could apply when the planet is closely connected with the question; for example, if it is in the house of the quesited.

We shall now consider the effects of the other classical planets in quick succession. Actually, it is not hard to interpret them if we bear the following in mind: the matters and persons symbolized by these retrograde planets cause or meet with reverses, delays, and difficulties, or are substandard in some way. Externally, the action of a retrograde planet is inhibited.

A **retrograde Saturn** is very often an indication of delays and obstructions. Often, little cooperation may be expected from official bodies such as the government or the civil service. If we are starting something new, we should be well advised to pay extra attention to the form, structure, and strength of that thing. A retrograde Saturn can introduce weakness or difficulties. With effort, such difficulties can be overcome, although a retrograde Saturn in any inception (or event) chart will always suffer from problems and setbacks.

Seen in this light, a **retrograde Jupiter** in a horary chart is not beneficial in questions relating to starting or completing higher education or special studies, travel to foreign countries and the like. Jupiter is the planet of expansion, but during its retrograde motion there is no provision for expansion in external matters. If we try to increase, enlarge, or expand when Jupiter is retrograde, little good will come of it. Thus, in event or inceptional charts, the success of a political party or politician starting a campaign under a retrograde Jupiter will not be great, and even a lost election is not unlikely. When a coup is engineered and Jupiter is retrograde, the new leaders will not hang onto power long. Jupiter retrograde hinders the necessary extension of their power-base. And if a singer or a pop group starts an important tour under a retrograde Jupiter, the tour will probably fail to contribute to their popularity.

So, in external matters—in the horary chart—Jupiter may withhold its benevolent action, although in natal charts it can be very helpful regarding situations concerning inner development. The big question is what we regard as inner and what we must regard as outer. Study, with a view to spiritual enrichment, belongs to the inner department of life. Yet a retrograde Jupiter seems to indicate problems when such study is undertaken: perhaps because philosophical study inevitably leads to social—that is to say, external—effects. However, where the study consists of self-tuition, and is not directed or tested by an outside body, but is motivated by the need for spiritual and intellectual development starting from within, a retrograde Jupiter is very valuable. For then the planet has a chance to express its urge for expansion inwardly, seeing that its external action is concealed.

Mars symbolizes action, energy, a love of doing things, enterprise, and so on. When Mars turns retrograde, its external action is inhibited. It so happens that, with a retrograde Mars, we often need to attempt all sorts of things. However, these things tend to be left unfinished or are spoiled by our impatience or rashness. Rashness is a danger, even with a direct Mars; and it becomes an even greater danger when the planet is retrograde, because a retrograde Mars temporarily loses its positive action on the external plane. All positive expressions of Mars are usually unnoticed. Thus, if we start a new job when Mars is retrograde, we can work as hard as we like but it will not be noticed, or we are undervalued, or our possibilities of demonstrating what we can do are limited. Activities we engage in threaten to go wrong or else make no impression on anyone. This means that if a government takes office during a retrograde period of Mars, it will suffer one setback after another, because every decision and every piece of legislation runs into opposition and delays. We should never accept administrative responsibilities when Mars is retrograde, for there will be considerable resistance to what we are doing and others will tend to think we are pretty useless, however good our intentions and however well we may seem to do in retrospect.

Mars symbolizes the beginning of things, initial action; and, when Mars is retrograde, this is a negative indication for the party or person who takes the initiative. Thus, if one country declares war on another during a retrograde Mars, the aggressor will lose (however long the war lasts). If you sue somebody while Mars is retrograde, you have a big chance of losing the case. But if someone else brings an action against you, it is unlikely to succeed.

When retrograde, Mars (more than any other planet) tends to create trouble. This is because it has to do with blood, quarrels, sharp instruments, accidents and similar things. A retrograde Mars in the horary chart for an operation can indicate excessive blood loss. In general, it is not advisable to undergo surgery during a retrograde Mars. Then the advice of horary specialists is to operate only in emergencies. However, a retrograde Mars is not a sign of death: other indications are necessary for this.

Danger of bloodshed is present when Mars is retrograde in the horary chart cast for the purchase of a car. Such a car often seems unusually prone to accidents; which, if not serious, can leave it covered in small dents. We should never enter a motor race with a retrograde Mars in the chart, because however well the car may perform, our luck in other respects could easily run out. Whatever the vehicle, there is more risk than usual of a collision, skid, or breakdown at this time with retrograde Mars.

Owing to the strong affinity between Mars and trouble, it is better to postpone a wedding if Mars is retrograde; otherwise the union may be full of strife. But it must be clearly understood that a marriage horoscope (cast for the moment the words "I do" are pronounced) is not sufficient grounds for predicting inevitable misery! Two people are involved who can learn a lot about understanding and managing their relationship without recourse to drama. Therefore there is no need to be worried by such an event chart, unless the partners are not prepared to see things from both sides, but always blame each other. In this case, retrograde Mars will do a great deal of harm. Sometimes, retrograde Mars in a marriage horoscope points to sexual problems.

If we wish to undertake a really important activity, then a retrograde Mars should be seen as an unmistakable warning of difficulties, certainly when the chart is for the commencement itself. Electional astrologers regularly advise against moving house, taking long journeys, signing business agreements and so on, during the retrograde periods. As far as accepting public office is concerned, I can only repeat that to do so when Mars is retrograde means walking into a big heap of trouble. In countries where violence and disturbances are everyday occurrences, a retrograde Mars may even carry the threat of assassination. What retrograde Mars is saying is: "Finish what you are already doing, and begin nothing new until I turn direct."

A **retrograde Venus** is a problematical indication when we want to know whether a love affair will lead to marriage; the external form is always inhibited. But if the question concerns a marriage and the querent genuinely wants to preserve the relationship, a retrograde Venus can offer encouragement. Venus benefits the old situations, but is a difficult factor where new situations are in view. Firm friendships also belong to Venus. Venus represents our affections, and we are not promised much in the way of new friendships when Venus is pulling back (retrograde).

A diplomat who has to enter into negotiations during a retrograde Venus will find it hard going, for the retrograde motion always gets in the way of outward success. This means that there is a great likelihood that the conference will come to a deadlock, that talks will be broken off, diplomatic relations severed, or peace treaties torn up. And, even if agreement is reached, the danger remains that it will not be kept, or that later on one or both of the parties will want to renegotiate or modify the pact.

Venus also concerns social events and the smooth running of meetings (Venus as ruler of Libra) and the like. If you are organizing a grand function in aid of something or other, and Venus is retrograde at the moment you decide to do so, or at the moment preparations begin, or at the opening of the function itself, then there is a greater chance of hindrances and letdowns; or of a certain stiffness because people will not throw themselves into the spirit of the thing.

But Venus as ruler of Taurus has still another side—that of money and legal currency. An administration that is inaugurated during a retrograde Venus may face serious financial problems. Sometimes devaluation of the currency is in the cards, or there are taxation difficulties, or financial fraud (e.g., counterfeit notes in circulation), and so on.

If we ask a question on our own account over the borrowing of money, then retrograde Venus puts an oar in the water to make sure the bank or other institution is not very helpful.

If, without any hidden motives to become a success, you take up some artistic pursuit to express your feelings—for example, painting, drawing, sculpting, flower arranging—then a retrograde Venus can give you a great deal of personal enjoyment in what you are doing without anyone else participating in it.

Another influence on the chart, very like the influence of Mars, is retrograde Mercury. As a planet relating to the mind and variability, it indicates that one or both of the parties will have frequent changes of mind on the subject in question, that a drastic review of policy will seem necessary, that there is a risk of misunderstanding, wrong interpretation, breach of contract, and so on. Sometimes, but by no means always, there is a chance that one of the partners in a contract is being fraudulent. Another quite common possibility is that, if the querent is symbolized by retrograde Mercury, he or she will have a change of mind about the query. A retrograde Mercury also suggests that problems can arise if we start something new, or put forward a new plan, try to renew something and so on—and this is wholly in keeping with theory.

Mercury has a lot to do with communication and trade, transfer and exchange, and with publishing houses, post offices, and so on. Therefore it is better to defer starting any of these enterprises as long as Mercury is retrograde. It is not so likely that the enterprise will succeed if it is launched during this period.

A retrograde Mercury is a really fine indication when the question is about missing documents, letters and so on, because it shows that they will come to light. And when we wish to hold a dialogue with ourselves, a retrograde Mercury helps here, too. The form of the dialogue hardly matters—this can be active imagination or what have you. During its retrograde motion, Mercury as a connecting factor gives us the chance to reintegrate various parts of our being, so we should take advantage of the period to get down to some serious self-examination. But any form of externalization involving others in the process, for example by starting therapy, will suffer from the limiting effect on contacts.

It can happen that Mercury turns retrograde within a few days of the question being asked; in which case, we very often see that, sooner or later, the querent has a change of mind, lets the matter drop, puts off dealing with the question, or something of the sort. Then we should look at Mercury's aspects in the chart, for these will tell us whether the changes made by the querent will be to his or her advantage or disadvantage.

• • •

As far as retrograde motion is concerned, we can study the planets both for what they are in themselves and also for what they are as house rulers—taking them in their latter capacity purely as significators of the quesited. If the indications given by significators make a horary chart very positive, but some planet naturally related to the subject is retrograde, there may well be delays or difficulties, but the further positive outcome is not cancelled.

Chart 3 on page 70 is the horary chart for the question: "Is it a good idea for me to sell my car and buy a new one?" The querent's car was in good running order and had only a small, constantly recurring fault. He was in a position to buy a newer, though second-hand, automobile, and the offer attracted him. The querent is symbolized by the 1st house. We find Capricorn on the Ascendant and Aquarius intercepted in the 1st. The significator of this man is, in the first place, Saturn (day ruler of Capricorn and night ruler of Aquarius). This is the classical planetary ruler. Those who want to work with the planets discovered more recently, can also use Uranus as his significator. As I have said elsewhere, the personal significators usually point to characteristics of the individual concerned, and in this instance the querent was an Aquarius, with a stellium in Capricorn in his radix.

The question concerned a car that was to be used as a means of transport. This is important to know, because when someone buys a car as a luxury item, for the sake of show, and as a status symbol, experience teaches us that it is a 9th house matter. But in this case it

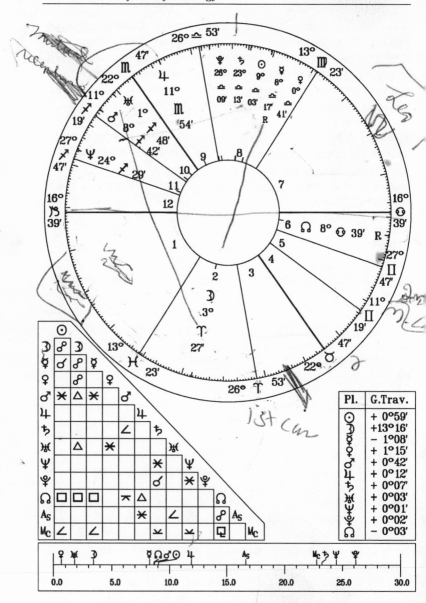

Chart 3. <u>Should I sell my car and buy a new one?</u> Amsterdam, Holland (52 N 22, 4 E 54), October 2, 1982, 2:18 P.M. GMT. Placidus houses. Chart calculated by Astrolabe, using *Nova Printwheels*.

has to be assigned to the 3rd house. The car's significator is Mars, because Aries is on the 3rd cusp. Since the question involves a sale and purchase, another party is involved, who will be found in the 7th house. This house has two rulers, and thus two significators, which are the Moon and the Sun. In order for a sale or purchase to take place, there has to be a connection between the significators of the querent and the other party. However, neither the Sun nor the Moon make any contact with Saturn. Now, if we look a long way ahead, we find that the Sun will transit Saturn before Saturn quits Libra. This could mean that a contact will take place leading to a successful transfer of ownership; but before that happens, the other significator of the other party, namely the Moon, is already in opposition to Saturn, the querent's indicator; which may mean that the transaction will not be completed.

If we take Uranus into consideration, we see that the Moon is making a separating trine to this planet, which shows that the contact over the offer has been agreeable to both parties. The Sun is separating from a much earlier sextile to Uranus, and this tells the same story. However, there is no new aspect to Uranus in the offing; which suggests that the sale will not be made.

The Moon poses something of a problem for the interpretation: it is co-significator for the querent, but also a significator of the other party. As co-significator of the querent, the Moon is forming a trine with Mars, ruler of 3, and therefore is significator of the querent's current car. The forming favorable aspect is a strong indication that the querent's current car will remain in his possession (incidentally, to his satisfaction). Now, if we take the Moon as significator of the other party, we must examine the situation of the other party by renumbering the houses. The 7th house becomes the 1st, the 8th becomes the 2nd (of the 7th) and the 9th becomes the 3rd (also of the old 7th). Thus the (old) 9th house (the new 3rd) represents the other party's car. The car looks good (Jupiter in 9), but apparently there is something more going on behind the scenes (Pluto on cusp 9). Venus, as the ruler of 9, is the significator of the other party's car, and we see that the Moon is separating from an opposition to Venus, a clear indication that the other party will wash his hands of the car. So we see how, by looking at the Moon in various ways, we obtain information about both parties.

When we have to choose between two objects, we set to work as follows. We look at the house in which the object of first choice falls →

in this case the current car—and then we go to the house that is as far removed from the object house as the object house is removed from the 1st house of the chart. In our example, the 3rd house represents the querent's car, so the 3rd house from the 3rd represents the other car. And the 3rd house from the 3rd is the 5th. Therefore the ruler of the 5th will be the significator of any new car, and this ruler is Mercury. Its motion is retrograde, which can indicate two things: that the car has hidden faults and/or that its sale will not be closed.

The Moon is approaching an opposition to retrograde Mercury—another sign that the car will not be purchased. That the querent's current car is still good, may be seen from this chart: the ruler of 3 is in 10, and therefore fortified, for planets in an angle are always powerful. What is more, it is in mutual reception with Jupiter. Mars is in Sagittarius, which is ruled by Jupiter, and Jupiter is in Scorpio, which is traditionally ruled by Mars; therefore we may treat Jupiter as if it were conjunct Mars, and vice versa.

The cost of running the car is represented by the 2nd from the 3rd house, i.e., the 4th house of the original chart. Venus is the ruler here, and Venus is in her own sign, and therefore strong. This has a positive meaning. That the Moon, as the significator of the querent, is in the process of leaving an opposition to Venus is again an indication that the querent wanted to part with his car because of anticipated costs.

It remains to look at the other car. Mercury, its significator, is retrograde—an ominous sign in itself. But Mercury is also combust (i.e., in close conjunction with the Sun), and is in the same degree as the North Node, and both factors warn against the proposed purchase. All in all, the horary chart clearly points to keeping the current car.

When I phoned the querent to inform him that I saw him keeping the car he had, he replied that the previous day he had decided not to sell it, for it was a vehicle that seldom or never let him down.

We have seen that the proposed new car can fall under two houses: the 5th as 3rd of the 3rd, and the 9th as 3rd of the 7th. Both houses supply information about the car, but the 5th tells us more about the attitude of the querent toward it, and the 9th tells us more about the attitude toward it of the other party. The combined information is generally very useful.

One last point on the retrograde motion in the chart may be worth mentioning. Mercury is also Lord of 8. The 8th house has to do with loans and credits. But Mercury is retrograde, and should the querent wish to borrow money to help pay for the new car, the retrograde Lord of 8 might make it difficult for him to raise some or even all of the funds required.

Stationary Planets

In the section on Retrograde Planets we saw that all the planets (not the Sun or Moon) appear to move backward in the zodiac for longer or shorter periods. Once their motion in a given direction, either direct or retrograde, is well established, they usually move quite quickly; but around the time when they change from direct to retrograde motion or vice versa, their speed is very slow and, at a certain point in the zodiac, they briefly come to a complete standstill. This standstill is interpreted in the wide sense of the word—a planet is said to be stationary when it covers a distance of less than one minute of arc per day. Stationary planets play an important part in horary charts for the following reasons:

• They are standing still, they cannot be applying by aspect to other planets. They can only be aspected by other planets. This means that a situation can arise in which the normally slow Pluto is forming an applying aspect to a stationary Mercury!

• They are devoid of motion, they seem like "blocks of concrete" that nothing can shift. You can not brush a stationary planet to one side; you must take notice of it. Such a planet makes its mark on the horoscope, especially when it is the significator of the querent or of the quesited. As a significator, a stationary planet indicates that the person it represents is displaying not the least flexibility or compliance in the matter concerned.

It is best to mark the symbol of a stationary, direct, and retrograde planet in the chart.

Refranation

Refranation happens when one of the significators is applying to an aspect with another significator, but leaves the sign or turns retrograde

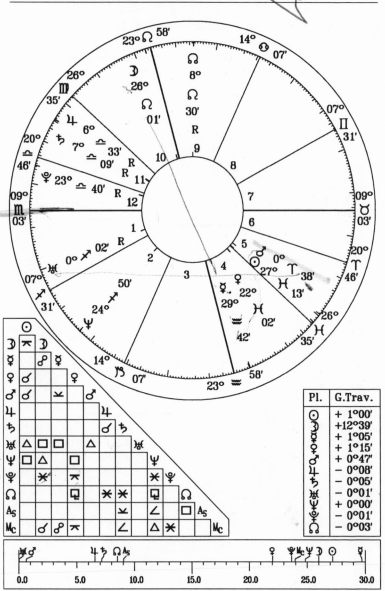

Chart 4. Will approval be granted? Amsterdam, Holland (52 N 22, 4 E 54), March 17, 1981, 9:44 P.M. GMT. Placidus houses. Chart calculated by Astrolabe, using *Nova Printwheels*.

before the aspect can be completed. In principle, this amounts to a situation where the swifter planet (which is always the starting-point in applying aspects) turns retrograde before the promised aspect is full, or where the slower planet leaves the sign before the swifter planet can make the aspect exact. In both cases, the event in prospect does not materialize.

When we are dealing with a planet that turns retrograde, then the party signified by the planet draws back. If there is a change of sign, the party signified has a radical change of mind, so that the matter undergoes, or appears to undergo, a complete alteration. Very often it simply means that everything is brought to a halt. With a significator that turns retrograde, the person signified is liable to leave the scene, either due to circumstances—sickness, accident, or something of the kind—or from personal choice. The precise reason is sometimes indicated by other aspects made by this planet.

Refranation can rob us of something to which we were looking forward; but, by the same token, it can avert a threatened calamity. Thus we must not regard it as something bad.

But now we come to Chart 4. The querent is an enthusiast for various forms of yoga, so much so that he has become an instructor. He has the most ambitious plans: at the very least he intends to found a big yoga institute; and not only wants recognition within yoga circles, but also seeks ministerial sanction. Obviously, he will have to file an application for this. While he was explaining his hopes and schemes to me, he suddenly broke off to ask, "Do you think approval will be granted?" Immediately I looked at the clock.

The chart presents the following picture. The man's significators are Mars (the traditional ruler of Scorpio), Uranus (planet in the 1st house) and, for those who like to include the trans-Saturnian rulers, Pluto. The Moon is co-significator. Mars is posited in 0° Aries, representing the querent's enthusiasm, pioneering spirit, and need to start something new. The 0° itself shows that the idea is recent and that this man has only just proceeded to action.

Where in the chart should we assign the approval he seeks? Two things are required to gain it: the passage of his application through the bureaucratic mill, and the decision of the ministry itself. The part played by official procedures falls under Virgo and its ruler, Mercury, and under the 6th house. The ministerial decision falls under the Sun (government) and under the 10th house (ruled here by the Sun). But Saturn, too, can have a finger in the pie.

The man's significator, Mars, also rules the 6th. This is a powerful combination and, in itself, would show that he has the matter well under control; but Mars is in the process of forming oppositions — not a favourable indication, either for the querent or in regard to the smooth-running of the official procedures. What is more, Saturn is retrograde — which discourages one from being too hopeful about the outcome of the ministerial deliberations. Nothing is going to be done quickly.

The man's second significator is Uranus, and this is retrograde; which could mean that he, himself, is not doing enough. Also, with Uranus in the 1st, we must expect the unexpected, and it is quite likely that the querent will do something unpredictable, or will change his mind; not a very positive sign.

The Moon is in the 10th house. This complicates the issue, because the Moon is both the co-significator of the querent and the significator of official approval of the project. Since it is applying to an opposition of Mercury, a planet that has to do with the administrative side of the question, the signs are not very propitious: they suggest that, however hard he tries, the man is fated to suffer from setbacks, high costs, or something similar. However, before the Moon's aspect to Mercury can become exact, Mercury slips out of Aquarius into Pisces. So the aspect fails to take effect (refranation). In fact, this is an example of a Moon void of course (see the relevant section), which usually means that nothing more happens. And so things appear to have turned out: the man has never taken steps to apply for recognition, but he has in fact built up a flourishing yoga practice. If, at first sight, this seems rather strange with the given horoscope, we must remember that we always have to work within the limits of the question without trying to deduce anything else from it. The question put to me was concerning official approval or recognition and had nothing to do with the success or otherwise of the yoga school; therefore the horary chart can tell us nothing about the latter. And here lies the danger: we are always inclined to read more into a horary chart than the simple answer to the question that was asked.

Although the following phenomenon rarely occurs, it is worth bearing in mind. It can happen that there is no promising aspect in the offing, because no further aspect appears to be due before the Moon enters the succeeding sign. But, during the short time the Moon traverses the last little bit of the sign she is in, another planet can back into its sign by retrograde motion, and the Moon can then aspect this planet before changing sign. If the planet is a significator of the quesited, this is naturally important. In the 1980s for example, Uranus, Neptune and Pluto were hovering around the end of one sign and the beginning of the next. If, at the time of a question, Uranus is at 0° Sagittarius and is the significator of the quesited, and if the Moon is at 3° Cancer, then there is no positively indicative aspect between the two. But should Uranus move retrograde into Scorpio before the Moon leaves Cancer, then a trine is formed between the two significators in the nick of time (the Moon is always co-significator of the querent), and that certainly is a positive indication. A situation can seem to be hopeless, but then there is a dramatic improvement. And yet, the significator of the quesited is in fact moving retrograde, and so everything will not come up to expectations or work out as planned and desired, and the piece of good luck can be accompanied by disappointments. Nevertheless, as in other cases of retrograde motion, this is very fortunate for a return to old conditions, for reunions, or for the return or discovery of lost or missing articles.

There is no name for this phenomenon, probably because it so seldom occurs; but it is certainly an important factor in interpretation when it does occur, and we should remember it as a variety of refranation.

Fixed Stars

The fixed stars form relatively stable patterns in the sky. They were given this name in antiquity to distinguish them from those heavenly bodies that undergo obvious changes in their relative positions: the Sun, Moon and planets. Although even the fixed stars have a proper motion (as it is called — as distinct from the circling motion they make *en masse*) the annual extent of the latter is so small that they look as if they are firmly set in place on the inside of the sky's rotating sphere.

The fixed stars have been used in astrology as far back as we have any knowledge of the art, although opinions still differ as to whether or not they have any value. In one book their use is encouraged, while in another they are totally ignored. Books on horary astrology are no exception to this rule. Some astrologers do without the fixed stars or even deliberately reject them, while others employ them regularly in preparing their interpretations.

The number of stars is unimaginably great, and more are continually being discovered. Obviously, we can not use them all—the horoscope would be absolutely peppered with them. If we use any at all, then they have to fulfill one or two qualifications; the most important being that they must belong to the brightest stars and be visible to the naked eye. The brightness of a star is expressed in magnitude. The fainter the star the higher the magnitude number. We can observe stars to the sixth magnitude with the naked eye; binoculars are needed to see stars of higher magnitude than this. Astrologers who work with fixed stars usually confine themselves to the very brightest.

Even when the above stringent requirements are met, the number of fixed stars eligible for use is still large. Their influences are expressed in terms of the characteristics of the planets. Thus, Arcturus is said to have the nature of Mars and Jupiter combined, and so on. These planetary combinations are merely signposts to the area in which the significance of the fixed stars has to be sought. A considerable amount of lore concerning some of the fixed stars has been gathered down the centuries. Interestingly enough, there are fixed stars of the sixth magnitude that do not have meanings assigned to them, nor are they all used. The reason for this we can only guess.

Frankly I do not use the fixed stars very often when I look at a horary chart, usually because a horary is usually easy to understand without using them. Sometimes, especially in cases of mundane or political events, a certain fixed star on the Midheaven or Ascendant gives extra weight to the delineation because it is so in line with what happens. Wim van Dam has written a handbook (in Dutch) for fixed stars with an excellent ephemeris; I'm sure that English speaking readers will find their own publications that will help locate the fixed stars. The fixed stars move slowly, but ten years can make a slight difference, so when I use them, I check the ephemeris to see if there is one on an important placement in the chart. The danger of working with fixed stars is that students may use positions "forever," not realizing that these positions change. Students should become familiar with the brightest of the stars, at least for the purpose of research.

If we intend to use the fixed stars, it is better to take two small an orb rather than one that is too large. A half or one degree is usual, but very bright stars may perhaps be allowed an orb of one-and-a-half degrees, and the brightest of all two degrees. It is for each of us to decide how far the fixed stars are useful.

Combustion

When a planet is posited in the same sign as the Sun and is less than 8½° away from the Sun, it is said to be combust. Combustion implies that the action of the planet is weakened. It is not much good for the question, and can hinder its progress. However, if the Sun or the combust planet is the significator of the querent, the combust planet loses its negative characteristics. Some astrologers maintain that the same is true when the Sun or the planet is a significator of the quesited, but opinions are strongly divided on this.

Even when a planet is somewhat further away from the Sun, there is still a state of combustion in a less intense form. The orb is as much as 17° and extends across cusps. If the significator is within 17° of the Sun, its strength is somewhat vitiated. We say that it is "under the Sun's beams." But opinions are strongly divided on this point, too, and many astrologers no longer pay it attention. In any case, a planet within 17° of the Sun is less visible than normal, and it is by analogy that the planet is said to have a less positive effect on the question being asked. Quite a few horary astrologers do not regard this as a negative indication; and some who pay regular attention to combustion and to planets "under the Sun's beams," will tell us that it should not be assumed that a planet less than 17° away from the Sun, or rather within 8½° of it, will display the traditional negative effect.

A third unfavorable place is the so-called Via Combusta, or the Burning Way, that part of the Zodiac lying between 15° Libra and 15° Scorpio. In the past, many difficult fixed stars stood here, but they departed a long time ago with the precession of the equinoxes. Spica and Arcturus, regarded as favorable stars, now occupy 23° and 24° Libra, and these two degrees are not treated as part of the Via Combusta. If a significator stands in the Burning Way, it is said to be debilitated. For further information, see chapter 3, section 5, where we have already discussed this topic.

Collection of Light

It sometimes happens in a horary chart that the significators of the querent and of the quesited, or of two parties, do not make any aspect to one another. In principle, this is a negative indication: no contact takes place and the querent fails to get what he or she wants. An exception is when the significators both make an applying aspect to a third planet which has to be the slowest of the three, otherwise the others could not apply to it. This third planet can represent a third person to whom both parties can turn and through whom they can make contact with one another. Such a role may be played, for example, by a realtor in the sale and purchase of a house. In this situation the answer can be completely positive. We say that the third planet collects the light from the two significators and so gets things "off the ground."

The third planet can also represent a certain favorable situation, but then there is always a person or group of persons creating the favorable situation (for example, a governmental decision) and promoting the indirect contact. For further information concerning the who and what, we must look at the house rulership of the third planet and see which house it occupies.

Neither translation of light nor collection of light are encountered very often; they are exceptions. But because they radically alter the result of the chart, we must always look to see whether or not they are present.

Exaltation and Fall

As we have already seen in the section on Debility, a planet occupying a sign that is alien to it can do little for the question. A planet in its own sign, on the other hand, can express itself naturally, and is in a good position to help the querent. But when it is in the sign opposite its own, it finds itself inhibited. For example: Mars rules Aries, but when in Libra (the sign opposite Aries) this planet of egocentricity, energy, and aggression is placed in a setting where concern for others, some self-indulgence, a love of fair play, and a willingness to compromise are prominent. Therefore Mars must, so to speak, waste a lot of energy in overcoming the Libran resistance to the expression of Martian spontaneity. Therefore, it has much less energy than usual to devote to the (possible) promotion of the matter. A planet that is posited, like this, in the sign opposite its own sign, is said to be in its detriment.

Exaltation and fall are terms that are a part of traditional astrology. These terms show where a planet is uncomfortable (fall) or comfortable (exaltation), with predictable results on its behavior. However, the rules are reliable only for the classical planets—Uranus, Neptune, and Pluto are still the subjects of debate when it comes to where they are well or poorly placed. Table 4 on page 82 shows how these work.

The planets Uranus, Neptune, and Pluto remain in the same sign for a long time, and present the same sign placement in horary charts for years at a time. Therefore there is little point in looking at their background when answering highly personalized questions. The trans-Saturnian planets are too collective to help with such details. Accordingly, the classical rulers of Scorpio, Aquarius, and Pisces are mentioned in the above scheme. I would also remark that Nicholas de Vore states his conviction (shared by others) that Mercury is exalted in Aquarius and in its fall in Leo, and I must say that I concur in this.[9]

As we have already seen, a planet posited in a sign opposite its own sign is said to be in its detriment. It has to express itself in a sign with characteristics that are opposed in important respects to those of its own sign.

The sign in which a planet is in its fall makes it difficult for it to be itself. For example, consider the active, energetic, and enterprising Mars—when in Cancer it generally encourages secondary reactions but not the taking of vigorous measures. Mars has a hard time deploying its forces; it is in its fall. Opposite the planet's fall is the sign of its exaltation. This is the other side of the coin again. Mars can certainly deploy its energy in Capricorn. Capricorn natives are usually hard workers, whose expectant attitude does not prevent them from being very businesslike as a rule. The undisciplined brute force of Mars, is given a direction, a goal, enabling it to accomplish a great deal. So what we have is the following:

---

[9]Lilly (op. cit., p. 104), quoting Ptolemy, gives Virgo as the exaltation of Mercury and Pisces as its fall. These attributes are still quoted in astrology books today. The author's concept is not classical teaching and has few adherents, so students may want to explore this further.

• A planet in its own sign can be completely itself and can develop its full potential, giving its utmost to the matter in hand;

• A planet in the sign opposite its own sign is in its detriment and can contribute little to the matter in hand;

• A planet also usually has a sign in which it can largely be itself; a sign, moreover, that adds an extra quality that gives a positive dimension to its action. This is its exaltation. Thus, Mars can exploit its energy in a more controlled way in Capricorn, Saturn gains in sociability from its placement in Libra, the Moon's action is more stable and less uncertain when it is in Taurus, and so on. On the same principle, Mercury could well have its exaltation in Aquarius, which would reduce the fickleness and add depth to the thought.

• The sign opposite the exaltation-sign is the sign in which a planet is in its fall; which is rather similar to being in its detriment, because here, too, it is at odds with its background and can do little good.

Table 4. Planets in Detriment, Exaltation, and Fall.

Planet	Own Sign	Detriment	Exaltation	Fall
Sun	Leo	Aquarius	Aries	Libra
Moon	Cancer	Capricorn	Taurus	Scorpio
Mercury	Gemini Virgo	Sagittarius Pisces	— —	— Virgo
Venus	Taurus Libra	Scorpio Aries	Pisces —	Virgo —
Mars	Aries (Scorpio)	Libra (Taurus)	Capricorn —	Cancer —
Jupiter	Sagittarius (Pisces)	Gemini (Virgo)	Cancer —	Capricorn —
Saturn	Capricorn (Aquarius)	Cancer (Leo)	Libra —	Aries —

Some authors restrict exaltation, fall, and detriment to certain degrees of a sign. I am still in the dark over the reason for this; there are no convincing astrological arguments either for or against it. What is certain, however, is that a planet is more at home in some signs than it is in others—a fact that must surely speak in favor of the broader view.

In horary astrology, it seems that when the significators are strong, the person is also strong or powerful—in other words the placement is positive. But, if one or more significators are debilitated, that is a negative indication. This can be applied in various ways. Let us suppose that the significator of the querent is weak; he or she will not be strong enough to bring about or carry through what is desired. And, if it is the significator of the quesited that is weak, the result fails to come up to expectations. Thus we may wish to buy something, but the weak placement of the significator of our intended purchase warns that the latter is likely to be in a bad state of repair. This is not necessarily unfortunate; someone with manual skills who buys second-hand items to repair them for resale will not worry about wear and tear if the price is low. I mention this to show that the context of so-called negative indications must always be studied, so that they can be assessed from the point of view of the querent.

Another situation in which a planet is strengthened is when it is in an angle. This is called an accidental dignity. It is then thought to be able to do more for the matter than it could do in the other houses. However the background influence of the sign must also be taken into consideration.

Peregrine

A planet is peregrine when it is in a sign where it has no essential dignity according to the rules of exaltation and fall. It is in an estranged or neutral position, being neither strong on the one hand nor bad on the other. For example, the Moon is peregrine in Libra. The Moon is domiciled in Cancer, is in its detriment in Capricorn, is exalted in Taurus and in its fall in Scorpio. In Pisces (the remaining water sign), the relationship with Cancer via the water element gives the Moon adequate opportunities to express itself in its own fashion. But Libra is a sign in which the Moon feels out of place, although there is no threat to the way it expresses itself; Libra is just usually alien territory.

In character interpretation today, we do not make so much use of exaltation, fall, detriment, and peregrine; and peregrine in particular is gradually being consigned to oblivion. But in horary astrology these factors are all still very much in evidence. If a planet is peregrine it is somewhat detached from the question. It is neither strong nor weak and so can do little to help or harm. When a peregrine planet is in reception, it loses its peregrine quality.

Now a planet that is unaspected contributes little to the question, for lack of useful outlets. And a planet that does not rule over any other planet is unable to initiate anything via dispositorship; hence the old adage that it is "of little value in the question."

Some people will question what I mean by an unaspected planet in the horary chart. I consider it to be unaspected when it does not have a major aspect within a 6° orb (4° if a sextile). For the Sun and Moon the orb is allowed to be 6° if either light forms a sextile, and 8° if they form other aspects to other planets. If one wants to consider inconjuncts (and not everyone does in horary astrology), the orb would be 3°. If planets don't fall into some kind of relationship with the orbs mentioned here, I consider them to be unaspected.

If the astrologer's own significator (the ruler of 7 if the question has been asked by someone else, and the ruler of 1 if it has been asked by the astrologer) is peregrine, this may mean one of several things: the astrologer may have failed to grasp the significance of the question, or may have gained a false impression of the circumstances of the case, so that the answer is wide of the mark; or the astrologer makes a mistake in interpretation, or the client misunderstands what is said, or disregards the astrologer's advice, and so on. Anyway, with a peregrine significator, things are not always what they seem, so we must be careful not to jump to conclusions.

For my own part, I have never observed bad effects associated with planets in neutral signs (such as the Moon in Libra in our example), provided there are no other difficulties in the chart. On the other hand, an unaspected planet as significator is troublesome in practice. The rule needs careful handling.

Frustration

We speak of frustration when two significators (one of the querent and one of the quesited) are forming a harmonious aspect with one another, or are moving toward a conjunction; but, before the aspect is exact, a third planet makes a disharmonious aspect with one of them. This third planet represents a third person or a situation that inhibits or prevents the promised good. But note well: this third planet produces a frustration only when it makes a tense aspect![10] The source of the trouble is sometimes to be found in the nature of the planet, but more often in the house it rules or in the house it occupies. Thus, the Lord of 2 can signify financial difficulties that ruin an undertaking.

When I was visiting with some married friends of mine, a phone call came for the husband. It was from a colleague with whom he was working closely on a scientific project. The colleague informed him that he had just been speaking with a scientist from America, who was very interested in the progress of the project; and, because our friend played an important role in it, the American intended inviting him to the States to give a series of lectures on his special field. Our friend made a note of the time when the invitation was extended and asked me if I would draw up a horary chart for it and tell him what this revealed. Now, we have to be very careful how we assign the houses, because a point arises that always requires watching: our friend certainly asked us a question, but our concern is not his request, "Can you do a horary chart for this?" but the moment when he was given the invitation over the phone. Therefore we must cast not a "question chart" but an "event chart." In such a chart, the person who takes the initiative is in house 1 and the person who received the phone call is in house 7. Our friend is in house 7, so we have to renumber the houses so that 7 is now 1. See Chart 5 on p. 86.

Next, we have to consider which other houses are important. Lectures can be ruled by different houses. The factual imparting of knowledge belongs to the 3rd house; expounding its meaning belongs to the 9th; however, a house that is often overlooked where lectures are

---

[10] I just want to stress that frustration comes from what we call tense aspects. There is always the possibility that events will take another course when there is a harmonious aspect to another planet first, but this aspect can also turn out to be very helpful in the long run. Experience shows me that only the hard aspects give frustration.

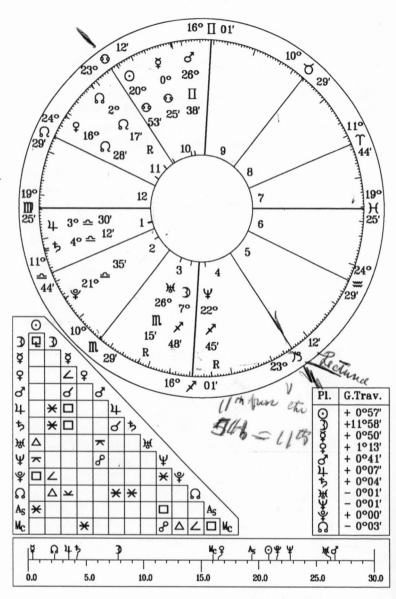

Chart 5. Event chart for an invitation. Amsterdam, Holland (52 N 22, 4 E 54), July 13, 1981, 9:15 A.M. GMT. Placidus houses. Chart calculated by Astrolabe, using *Nova Printwheels*.

concerned is the 11th. Congresses come under Aquarius, Uranus and the 11th house! My first inquiry was about the sort of meeting being convened for his lecture or lectures and what the object of them was. If he was simply making a factual report to his American fellow-scientists, we would have to look at the 3rd house. If the emphasis was going to be placed on his personal view of the subject, then the 9th house would play the main role. But, if he was attending a congress, the house to consider would be the 11th. I discovered that it was intended to organize a congress in which our friend would give at least one, and preferably several, lectures. So I took the 11th house of the renumbered chart, and that is the 5th house of the original chart.

Capricorn is on the cusp (of this new 11th, old 5th, house), so Saturn is the ruler. The friend himself is symbolized by Jupiter as the classical ruler of Pisces, and possibly by Neptune. There is a magnificent indication in the horoscope: in the house that represents meetings (house 7 in the renumbered chart), Jupiter and Saturn are conjunct, and Jupiter is making the aspect exact. Our friend had made up his mind to accept the invitation.

But before Jupiter reaches the place of Saturn, Mercury makes a square, first to Jupiter and then to Saturn. The journey did not take place, the congress was never held. Why was that? To answer this, we must look at the situation as shown in the renumbered chart. For our friend, the scientist from America was the "other party," who falls in the 7th house of the renumbered chart. Virgo is on the cusp here, so Mercury is the significator of the other party. What the chart is telling us is that the person who extended the invitation would himself prevent it from bearing fruit. And this is what seems to have happened. The man found it difficult to get on with others and, right from the start, he put so many people's backs up that his plans were wrecked. He was over-ambitious, and his professional reputation had already suffered some damage. In this connection, take a look at Mercury as the Lord of 10 for the other party; it stands in 10 (the professional sphere). Through the square it makes, it becomes a source of trouble.

The Moon Void of Course

We say that the Moon is void of course when it makes no further major aspect before leaving the sign in which it is posited. The moment the Moon becomes void of course is the moment when its last major aspect is exact. Generally, the Moon is void of course in the last degrees of a sign. But if the situation is such that all the planets occupy the first degrees of signs, the Moon's last major aspect will be made early on and it will be void of course for quite a period. On the contrary, if many planets occupy the ends of signs, the Moon will make her last major aspect late and the period during which she is void of course is very short, provided, of course, a *major* aspect can be formed.

In order to tell when we are working with a Moon void of course, it is helpful to have an ephemeris that gives the daily aspects with their Greenwich Time, and the moment when the Moon enters a new sign. In *The American Ephemeris* there is a daily aspectarian and a special column for lunar phenomena, giving the moment when the last aspect is exact and the moment when the Moon enters a new sign. Such a column can look like this:

Void of course Moon January 1983

Last Aspect		Moon Ingress		
2	8 P.M. 39	2	♍	9 P.M. 50
4	11 P.M. 01	5	♎	0 A.M. 45
7	6 A.M. 03	7	♏	7 A.M. 17
9	4 A.M. 17	9	♐	5 P.M. 14
12	4 A.M. 15	12	♑	5 A.M. 27
14	5 P.M. 19	14	♒	6 P.M. 27

In the column "Last aspect" the day and the time in Greenwich Time are given for the moment when the last major aspect of the Moon in the sign it occupies is partile. Thus on January 2, 1983, this is at 8 hours 39 minutes in the evening (P.M.), or 20h 39m Greenwich Time. At this point the Moon goes void of course until it enters the next sign, which happens January 2, 1983 at 9 hours 50 minutes in the evening (P.M.), or 21h 50m Greenwich Time. So, in this case, the Moon is void of course for only a short time: 1 hour and 11 minutes to be precise. However, in other instances, the Moon is void of course for a whole day or even longer.

A Moon void of course has great consequences for horary interpretation. Its keyword is *nothing*. Nothing happens; and, if we bestow our best efforts on something, it is all for nothing. On making a list of various possible interpretations, we arrive at the following situations:

- The querent abandons the quesited;

- The querent stops dealing with the quesited;

- If the querent wishes to start something new, it comes to nothing;

- If the querent is ill, the illness does not get worse. In fact, because there is nothing to worry about, there may be a quick recovery;

- If something is lost or missing (a person, animal, or article), once more there is nothing to worry about. The lost article will be returned, the missing person or animal will come home;

- If the querent wants to take some initiative, it will do no good. Nothing he or she can do will alter the current situation; events will simply take their course;

- If the querent has a bright idea, it will remain a bright idea, and nothing more. To put it in a nutshell, when the Moon is void of course, there is a great deal of discussion this way and that, but no action.

Nevertheless, we need to be aware that there are several instances in which something can, in fact, occur. When the Moon is not a direct significator of the querent or the quesited but, as usual, just a co-significator of the querent, something may get off the ground in the following instances:

- When the significators of the querent and the quesited are firmly connected (for example by an applying trine or by reception) and are making a very promising aspect. These are extremely positive indications that the answer is yes. However, the Moon shapes events, and, if it is void of course when the situation is implicitly favorable, the worst that can happen is a delay (generally for one, two or three months). The Moon void of course is unable to stop them.

- When the Moon is within three degrees of making a major aspect after passing into another sign. Here, too, the effect of the Moon being void of course is weakened. Some horary astrologers reject this rule, while others maintain that the Moon is definitely no longer void of course when it is within three degrees of forming an aspect across a cusp. For example, if the Moon is 29° 14' Aquarius and void of course, and the next major aspect is to the Sun at 0° 55' Cancer: to form the

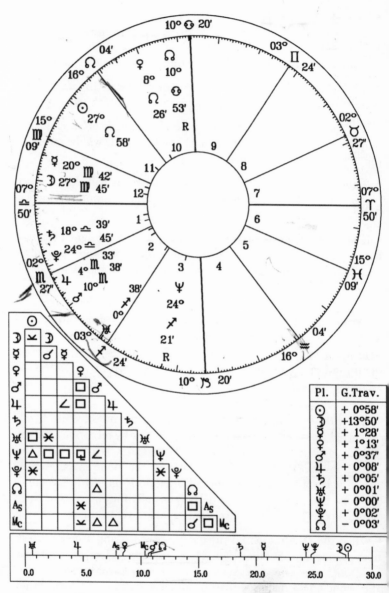

Chart 6. Will he buy the house? Amsterdam, Holland (52 N 22, 4 E 54), August 21, 1982, 8:28 A.M. GMT. Placidus houses. Chart calculated by Astrolabe, using *Nova Printwheels*.

aspect, the Moon must enter Pisces, but because the distance that has to be covered to make the aspect exact is less than three degrees, the void-of-course action is not so definite. My own experience shows that the void-of-course action does not entirely disappear in such a case. Something is certainly likely to happen, but *when* it will happen is not so certain; the pace of events is slowed down.

• When the Moon is void of course in Taurus, Cancer, Sagittarius, or Pisces, then, according to Lilly, action is certainly possible. Experience teaches that action is indeed possible with a Moon void of course in these signs, but it is not inevitable. Where precisely to draw the line between action and no action, you will have to determine with practice.

• When a Moon void of course is conjunct, sextile, trine, or parallel the Part of Fortune, we can generally rely on enjoying unqualified success. A development takes place. If there is a square or opposition to the Part of Fortune, some improvement always occurs, but at the cost of (considerable) loss.

It is not only the Moon that can be void of course; the planets, too, can be so placed that they have no further major aspect to make with a slower planet. We always consider the faster planet, because we are dealing with applying aspects. If a planet is void of course, the keyword "nothing" applies to it in the sense that there is nothing it can do. If it is the significator of the querent or of the quesited, this is a warning not to expect any results from the question.

Now let's look at Chart 6. A good friend phoned me enthusiastically with the news that he had seen a very desirable house for sale. It was just what he was looking for and, although it was in need of a certain amount of renovation and modernization, he had set his heart on it. Money was no problem. I wanted to know if he would really proceed to buy the house, so I made a note of the time of the announcement of his plans.

The Moon is at 27° 45′ Virgo and forms no further major aspects before leaving this sign; so it is void of course. In itself, this means, "all talk and no action;" but Uranus is 0° 38′ Sagittarius, and still within three degrees of a major aspect with the Moon. As soon as the Moon enters Libra it will sextile Uranus; and this means that the Moon is no longer void of course. But what actually happened? The matter began and ended with the one phone call. I have never heard this friend mention the house again, nor has he taken any steps to purchase it. This strongly suggests that the Moon remained very much in its void-of-course mode.

Possibly, the idea that the Moon can no longer be treated as void of course when it is within three degrees of forming an aspect after moving across a cusp, should be combined with Lilly's rule that the Moon can initiate action when it is void of course in Taurus, Cancer, Sagittarius, or Pisces. Some of my own results appear to point in this direction and might justify readers experimenting for themselves.

If we examine this horary chart more closely to obtain an answer to the question, we can proceed as follows. It was a query concerning a friend, therefore we must look at the 11th house. The cusp of that house is in Leo (my friend is a Leo!). We now treat the 11th house as the 1st house. Selling and buying are involved, and my friend was thinking of buying. The other party, the seller, is in the 7th house from the 11th, which is the 5th house of the original chart. The friend's significator is the Sun, and the ruler of the prospective seller is Saturn or Uranus. We must now inquire whether or not there is any aspect between the two significators. The Sun is 27° 58' Leo and Uranus is 0° 38' Sagittarius, so there is no major aspect between them. To be sure, in the future, as soon as the Sun crosses the cusp between Leo and Virgo, they will form a square; but is it allowable to attribute any effect to this square across the cusp? Once more, we have a void-of-course situation: from the point reached by the Sun in Leo, it makes no further aspects until it has left the sign. Yet Uranus is within three degrees of a major aspect with the Sun; so here again we are faced with the question whether or not the planet concerned (in this case the Sun) is still void of course. The fact of the matter is that my friend took no further action, he did *nothing*, which is characteristic of a void-of-course situation.

Because Saturn is in the 1st house of this chart, and I was the one who asked the question, Saturn warns of a possible error in interpretation. If I had applied the three degrees rule without further ado, I should have had to conclude that contact would take place between buyer and seller, because both Sun and Moon aspect Uranus across the cusp. One of the aspects was very promising (the sextile), the other pointed to problems (the square). The contact between buyer and seller was not going to be plain sailing. But this would have been to draw the wrong conclusion, for there was no contact at all, and no action was taken. (For the role this Saturn can play, see chapter 4.) Let us take extra care over rules with so-called exceptions!

7

START

Estimating Time

Although there are recognized rules for determining when certain things will happen, applying them is not always easy in practice! Sometimes we need to call on the help of our ingenuity and intuition. Estimating time is controversial, and to many it is a risky thing to attempt.

We plunge into difficulties as soon as we try to select a planet as starting point. It is customary to begin with the significator of the querent or, sometimes, of the quesited. But, if the querent's significator is retrograde or afflicted, it is not always usable for estimating time. And, when there is a problem such as this, the Moon is often chosen as the starting point; not only because it is co-significator of the querent, but because the Moon exerts a powerful influence on the way in which things happen.

First, we must note the type of house and sign occupied by the significator or by the Moon; for this determines the unit of time to be employed. In determining the times of events, we do not consider the speed of the planetary motions through the zodiac—as might have been expected—but the distance in degrees to the next positive contact between the (co-)significators of the querent and the quesited. Each degree represents a certain length of time, all according to the sign and house in which the Moon, or other significator used as our starting point, happens to stand.

If we start with the Moon, which is going to make an aspect with a significator of the quesited, then the house and sign in which it stands decides the unit of time. If we start from another planet as significator of the querent (which, in that case, must be forming an aspect with the significator of the quesited), then the house and sign of *this* planet decides the unit of time. The unit of time is ascertained from Table 5.

Admittedly, it is rather tricky to make the correct choice of time unit from among the possibilities; for one thing, the nature of the question has to be considered. If the query concerns an expected phone call, shorter time units are appropriate; if it concerns establishing a business, we need to think in terms of longer time units. Complicated lawsuits can take years to settle, and it may be wise to make the time units longer than usual. In short, common sense and intuition should be our guide in each instance.

Another point to bear in mind is that, in practice, it seems that a matter may well come to a head more quickly than expected when all the indications found are from cardinal signs and angular houses. In a case like this, we must be careful not to step down to a lower time unit than the ones given in the Table 5. We should simply reckon that the course of events will be accelerated. Suppose, for example, our initial calculation gives us a timing of six days, and all the indications are in

Table 5. Horary Units of Time.

Angles	Time Increments
Cardinal signs	Days or hours
Mutable signs	Weeks or days
Fixed signs	Months or weeks
Succedent Houses	Time Increments
Cardinal signs	Weeks or days
Mutable signs	Months or weeks
Fixed signs	Years or months
Cadent Houses	Time Increments
Cardinal signs	Months or weeks
Mutable signs	Years or months
Fixed signs	Unlimited length or years

cardinal signs and angular houses, we must not say that "therefore" the six days are really six hours! What we *are* entitled to say, however, is that events will take place some time between the fourth and the sixth day, and most probably around the fifth day. In other words, things will happen a little earlier than would otherwise have been expected, but still in the same time scale.

So what do we actually do to determine the time of an event? Here is the process, step by step:

A) Take the significator of the querent that is still going to make an aspect with the significator of the quesited; or else take the Moon, provided it is going to make an aspect with the significator of the quesited. Note: if no contact is due to take place, there is naturally no time to determine (no time is occupied by something that does not happen). We need an applying aspect between either the significator of the querent and that of the quesited, or the Moon and the significator of the quesited. If the querent's significator is retrograde, use the Moon.

B) Measure the distance in degrees to a partile aspect between the two significators, irrespective of whether it is a conjunction, a sextile or a trine. Thus, when one is at 14° Cancer and the other at 18° Pisces, the distance is 4°.

C) See in which sign and house the faster significator stands which will be used to determine the time; otherwise, in which sign and house the Moon stands. (As only the querent's significator, or the Moon, can determine the measurement, we must of course limit ourselves to these two, and not look at the significator of the quesited.) Now consult Table 5 for the time unit, and consider whether or not it is appropriate for the question.

D) The number of degrees difference multiplied by the chosen time unit indicates the time that will elapse before the event takes place. Thus, if the time unit is a month, a distance of 4° represents a period of four months.

Further problems can arise when we are working with a renumbered chart (see chapter 4). We may be faced by problems of choice: should we keep to the original houses, or should we take the angular, succedent and cadent houses as reckoned from the 1st house in the renum-

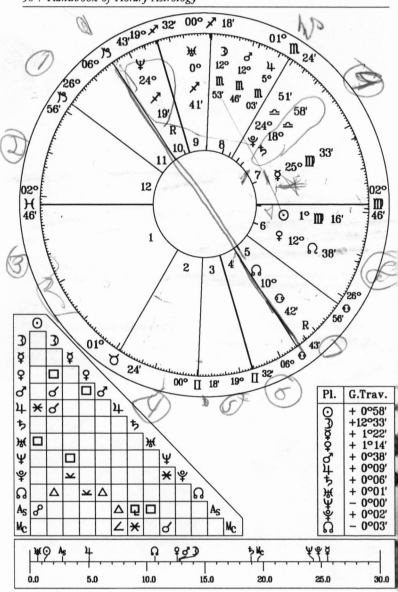

Chart 7. Will Fred stay in Australia, or will we meet again? Amsterdam Holland (52 N 22, 4 E 54), August 24, 1982, 6:44 P.M. GMT. Placidus houses. Charts calculated by Astrolabe using *Nova Printwheels*.

bered chart? It is not easy to give a clear-cut answer. I have seen both methods work in practice, but am of the opinion that the renumbered chart ought to be given preference.

Let us use Chart 7 as an example. A very dear friend left Amsterdam in August, 1982 to go to his Australian girl friend. In principle, he wanted to stay in Australia and marry her. This meant the loss of a good friendship for my husband and myself, and I wondered whether he would stay there or not. In the back of my head, I was simultaneously hoping that we were going to see him back home soon and that he would be happy overseas. A rather ambivalent attitude—but clearly defined! I kept on turning the whole situation over unconsciously in my mind until, suddenly, it gelled for me and I asked the question. This was the moment for which I cast the horary chart.

In the horary chart, the Ascendant is at 2° 46′ Pisces, which places a restriction on the interpretation. It suggests that the question was asked prematurely. But, meanwhile, Fred was well and truly in Australia, and it was not entirely clear to me what was too early about my question. I decided to take a closer look at the chart.

My own significators are Jupiter and Neptune, and Mars as Lord of Aries. Fred's significator is Saturn, because Capricorn is on cusp 11. The question had to do with his journey to a foreign country, therefore I renumbered the houses so that the 11th became the 1st. The 7th house then became the 9th of the 11th. We find his significator, Saturn, in his 9th house—he is abroad. Also, Mercury, the ruler of his 9th is in that 9th house, too. This is always a strong indication that something important faces the person concerned. Also, the ruler of his 10th house, Pluto, is in the 9th (at least if we treat Pluto as the ruler of Scorpio). He was keen to create an independent sphere of activity for himself in Australia. If we treat Mars as Lord of Scorpio, then, as Fred's ruler of the 10th house, we find it occupying the same 10th house. The foreign country is well to the fore in this chart.

Of my own significators, including of course the Moon as my co-significator, only Neptune is about to receive an aspect—a sextile from Saturn, Fred's significator. Neptune is retrograde: I am unable to intervene, all I can do is wait. There are 5° 21′ between 24° 19′ (Neptune) and 18° 58′ (Saturn). Let us return for a moment to the chart as it was before we renumbered it. Both Fred's significator and mine are angular; his is cardinal, mine is mutable. This points to a result within days or weeks. Since a mutable sign is on cusp 7 (the cusp of the house occupied by Fred's significator), we would expect to be looking at weeks rather than days; but, given the situation, this did not strike me as the most probable period. On looking once more at the renumbered chart, we find Fred's significator in his 9th house in a cardinal sign. A cadent house combined with a cardinal sign gives months. I decided, guided by the knowledge that the action had to come from him, to use months as the unit of time.

A difference of 5° 21' has then to be converted into some five months and ten days of time. The question was posed on August 24, 1982, thus around February 3, 1983, Fred might be expected either to make contact, or to come back. However, I was careful not to set my hopes too high. The degree on the Ascendant warned me that judgment was rather problematical. Be that as it may, on January 20, 1983, Fred suddenly appeared on our doorstep. He was home from Australia, earlier than the distance in degrees had led me to expect. The chart actually tells us why. Neptune, my significator, being retrograde, was moving in the direction of Saturn. When both planets are closing the gap between them, then the result is usually hastened a little. That was the case here.

Now what about the doubt hanging over the interpretation, suggesting that the question was premature? Fred and his girl friend had decided to marry not in Australia but in England, working there for a while and visiting friends. Then they wanted to stay for a long time in the Netherlands, before finally returning to Australia. Thus my question about a permanent residence in Australia was certainly asked too early!

What mattered in this chart were the angular, succedent, and cadent houses, reckoned from the 1st house of the renumbered chart.

Sometimes it is a good idea to use the transiting Moon to determine time. The Moon moves through one zodiac degree about every two hours. When we are dealing with a time unit of hours, the Moon can often help us pinpoint the exact time. Say a question is asked at 11:33 hours and the Moon is still 3° 30' short of forming a partile positive aspect with a significator. In principle, the event will take place seven hours after the question was asked, that is to say around 18:33 hours.

Often we are right on target, but there may be snags. Sometimes the time-unit-per-degree system works equally well. In the present case, if we were to take an hour for a degree, we should have to consider the event taking place in three and a half hours. There are no rules telling us when to use one method or the other. To some extent, we have to be guided by our feelings.

If we select the method where each degree traversed by the Moon is interpreted as two hours, then (according to tradition) we have to take into account the Moon's latitude (given in most ephemerides next to the column showing declinations). If the Moon's latitude is zero, we may accept the calculated time as correct. When the Moon has north latitude, things happen more quickly; and, at south latitude they happen more slowly.

Of course, we must never ignore what the rest of the horoscope has to say when we are judging the time element—especially if the angles are in cardinal signs and the significators are in angular houses. This always expedites the matter.

All sorts of variants have been devised for determining time. Some astrologers take the distance in degrees to an aspect between both significators, and theoretically this is the best method. The two significators in an applying aspect always give notice that something is going to happen, and the difference in degrees ought to supply the timing—or so one would think. Unfortunately, the method does not always give the right answer. Therefore, various attempts have been made to find other differences in degrees that can be employed as time measures. But these variants, too, have met with mediocre success and some seem to be absolutely useless.

Among the variants we can consider the distance to an aspect between: the significator of the quesited and the Moon; the cusp of the house representing the quesited and the Moon; the cusp of the quesited and the significator of the quesited; the cusp of the house of the quesited and the Lord of 1; the significator of the quesited and the degree of the Ascendant; it is very hard to choose from among all these. Although the above-mentioned rules do give us something to go on, they have lacunae that require solutions through intuitive decisions. Therefore, it makes sense to save all our horary charts so we can check them later to see which timing was right. This gives us first-hand material to see where we went wrong and why. Nothing could be more instructive!

Chart 8 on page 100 is an example showing that the significators can supply information on the timespan between the question and the event. This is an event horoscope. It is cast for the moment when we received a letter from the Amsterdam City Council asking us to make an appointment with a named social worker. Because of extensive

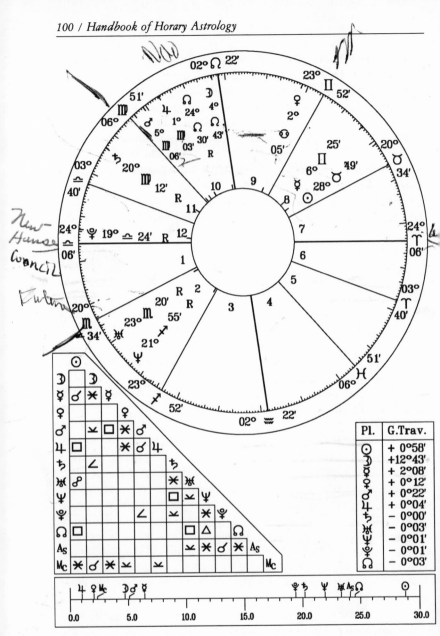

Chart 8. Event chart for moving to a new house. Amsterdam, Holland (52 N 22, 4 E 54), May 19, 1980, 4:09 P.M. GMT. Placidus houses. Chart calculated by Astrolabe using *Nova Printwheels*.

urban renewal in our district we were going to have to be rehoused. The object of the interview with the social worker was to discuss the type and situation of the new housing.

Since the Council took the initiative, it falls in the 1st house of the chart. We fall in the 7th house. Aries is on cusp 7, so our significator is Mars. The place where we were still living falls in the 10th house of this chart, because it is the 4th of the 7th. Our future residence accordingly falls in the 4th of the 4th of the 7th house, which is the 1st house of the original chart. Libra is on the cusp there, so Venus is the significator. We note that, in this chart, Venus is approaching a sextile with Mars. So both significators are linked harmoniously by an applying aspect—which places the event in the future. The distance between the two is 5° 05′ (Mars) – 2° 04′ (Venus) = 3° 01′, which we can treat as a fraction over three time units. Seeing that Venus, the significator of the new house, occupies a cardinal sign in a cadent house (both in the original and in the renumbered chart), we could be looking at a timespan of months or weeks. Given the time usually taken by bureaucratic procedures, months are the more likely; and this gives us a time of three months. The Council's letter arrived on May 19, so I anticipated that something would have to happen in regard to the rehousing near August 19. At noon on August 18, we took possession of the keys of our new house and, on August 19, we started to move in.

☙ I have included this chart because it doesn't really work and is a good example in itself. The sextile between Mars and Venus never becomes exact, because Venus is going retrograde. When I did this chart, I totally overlooked this. The response from the housing bureau did happen on May 18th as I have told you, and it was not until the editor of the English version of this book looked at the Venus placement did I realize that the aspect could not become exact. She wondered what had happened with the event.

Perhaps more background information is interesting to American readers. Every municipality in Holland has the right to assign rental houses to people because there is a shortage of housing here. There are a number of restrictions about this housing and it is difficult to get what you want. We were hoping that we could get a house that was large enough for my husband and myself and the children, and also have enough space to work at home. This was difficult because the social worker could not overcome the housing restrictions to get us the space we needed. The houses assigned by the municipality are ruled by

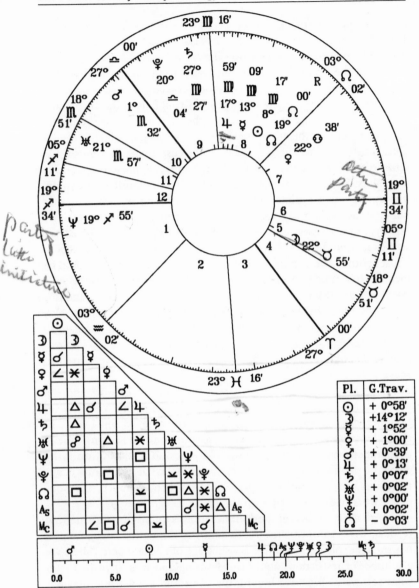

Chart 9. Signing of the agreement between the Polish Government and free trade union Solidarity. Gdansk, Poland (54 N 23, 18 E 40), August 31, 1980, 1:46 P.M. GMT. Placidus houses. Chart calculated by Astrolabe using *Nova Printwheels*.

the 4th house of the horary chart, and in this case, it is ruled by Saturn. The retrograde Saturn in the horary tells us that the house won't fit with our circumstances—it will be too small, or something will be wrong with it. This was actually the case. We moved into our new house, but it was small. We had no difficulty with the move, and we did not mind leaving our old neighborhood. We knew that living and working in the new house that was assigned to us would be impossible in the long run, so we decided not to invest much money in this move, as we knew that it would be best to wait for an opportunity that would eventually give us the space that we needed. The Moon on the 4th also indicates the short stay. In 1983 we moved to our new home, where we still live, and which allows us the space we need. So the horary chart, with Saturn in the 4th, was the indicator that something would not work out for us. Getting the letter told me that we would have to leave our old house fairly soon, which was true, and opening the letter actually indicated that we would move shortly. So in one way, the chart worked as an indicator of what happened!

Whenever, in a horary chart, we are concerned with matters that can hang fire for a long time, or take a long time to accomplish, it makes sense to pay attention to transits and secondary progressions too. If the question concerns something that could take years to resolve, then even primary directions can provide indications of the timing of events. My experience of the use of transits, secondary progressions or primary directions in horary charts is so positive, that I would advise everyone to keep and progress their horary charts. If several questions crop up in succeeding months, we progress the chart already cast for the matter in hand. This seems to give the best results. And sometimes the most useful course seems to be to combine progressions, transits and the distance in degrees between the significators.

This next chart is an example of progressions and transits in a horary chart. Chart 9 is the horoscope of the moment in Gdansk, Poland when the solemn signing took place of the agreement between the Polish government and the free trade union Solidarity. This led to legal recognition of the trade union and to the release of many political prisoners.

Houses 1 and 7 are always involved in contracts and agreements. The 1st house belongs to the party taking the initiative in the agreement. The other party has the 7th house. Mercury and the Lord of the 3rd house also play a part.

Solidarity is the party that took the initiative and is therefore represented by the 1st house. Jupiter is the significator of Solidarity, as is Neptune which is in the 1st house, also the Moon, of course, as co-significator. The government of Poland is ruled by the 7th house and its significator is Mercury, the Lord of 7, also Venus as a planet in 7, and also the Moon as Lady of the intercepted sign Cancer.[1]

It is immediately obvious that the chart holds a grave warning: Neptune in the 1st house suggests that things may not turn out as Solidarity expects, and that they have not judged the intentions of the other party correctly. But the chart contains other (hidden) warnings. Jupiter, the significator of Solidarity, and Mercury, the significator of the Government, are conjunct. In itself, this is very hopeful, but Mercury is clearly the stronger of the two. It is in its own sign, whereas Jupiter is in its detriment; thus the regime has Solidarity at a disadvantage. What is more, the two conjunct Significators are square retrograde Neptune in 1, which alerts us to the possibility of breach of contract, deception, chaotic events and so on. These dangers are impending because the square is not yet exact. To make matters worse, Neptune is in the same degree (of Sagittarius) as the North Node (Leo) — a further warning.

Jupiter plays a double role in this chart: it is the ruler of 1 and the traditional ruler of 3. Solidarity, accordingly, appears to be well placed to take advantage of the contract right from the start. However, Jupiter, as ruler of the 3rd house, is involved in an applying square to retrograde Neptune; so the contract may not be as ironclad as it should be. And we have already seen that Jupiter is in an uncongenial sign, suggesting that both Solidarity and the contract will run into difficulties. The Moon has one more aspect to make before she leaves Taurus, a trine to Saturn. Good though this is, it is not good enough to counterbalance the problems in the chart.

As we know, things did go wrong. Jupiter is 17° 59′ Virgo and Neptune 19° 54′ Sagittarius, a difference of 1° 55′. Translating this difference into years, we get a period of approximately two years. But since Neptune is retrograde and is therefore moving back toward Jupiter, the time is likely to be shortened. The solemn agreement was signed on August 31, 1980. Less then sixteen months later, in the dead

---

[1]Moon significator of Solidarity and Government. And, in 1989, of course, Solidarity became an important part of the Government. The conjunction of the two significators mentioned would also seem to reflect power-sharing. Trans. note.

of night on the 12th, or 13th of December, 1981, about 150,000 Solidarity members were arrested and, on October 2, 1982, some two years after the signing of the agreement, Solidarity was officially banned by the Polish parliament. Thus the difference in degrees does not supply us with a precise measure of time. But let us take a look at the transits, progressions, and primaries.

December 13, 1981

In primary directions we find the following major aspects:

Planet	Aspect	Aspect becomes Exact
Jupiter	square Ascendant	December 7, 1981
	square Neptune	March 2, 1982
Uranus	opposite Moon	December 3, 1981

About this time, the MC of the chart was making a semisquare to Mercury (partile on November 1, 1981). We know that a primary direction can color a long period, but certainly the months around the time when it is exact are important. Here there are several relevant primary directions of and to the significators of Solidarity—Jupiter, Neptune, and the Moon. These were involved in dangerous conflicts. The sudden character of the state of emergency declared on December 13, 1981 is strikingly shown by Uranus, which makes an opposition to the Moon.

The secondary progressions give no indications, but the transits do. The planetary positions for midnight (0:00 h) on December 13, 1981 (from the *American Ephemeris*) are:

Sun	20° 53′ 23″	♐	The Sun is Lord of 8 in the chart and has just crossed the Ascendant.
Moon	13° 59′ 39″	♋	Sextile the significator of the Government at midnight.

Mercury	22° 12' 08"	♐	Mercury, the significator of the Government, makes an exact yod here with the Moon and Venus, to each of which it forms an inconjunct. A yod is often dramatic in its effects.
Venus	2° 40' 00"	♒	It is also just over a degree beyond a square to Mars.
Mars	28° 34' 02"	♍	Just over a degree past an exact square to Saturn, the co-significator of Solidarity.
Jupiter	2° 59' 02"	♏	Exactly square cusp 8!
Saturn	20° 11' 04"	♎	Saturn, as co-significator of Solidarity, makes an almost exact conjunction with Pluto.
Uranus	1° 37' 04"	♐	
Neptune	24° 26' 02"	♐	
Pluto	26° 16' 03"	♎	Pluto is within a one-degree orb of the MC; an unmistakable indication of clandestine power struggles and open outbursts.
North Node (Mean)	24° 12'	♋	This is the mean position of the North Node. It shows nothing.
North Node (True)	22° 43'	♋	The True Node has reached the same number-degree as the number-degrees occupied by the Moon and Venus—significators of the two parties. A powerful warning! In addition, it is conjunct Venus, the significator of the Government.

Pluto remained for a whole month in 26° Libra, which means that it was on the MC for a month. When Pluto turned direct within a 1° orb of the MC, Solidarity was officially outlawed by the parliament of Poland on October 2, 1982.

In the transits listed here, the maximum orb is 1°. Hence in progressions and in transits, the aspects formed are quite close to exact and are obviously applicable.

8

Estimating
Place, Direction
and Distance

We are going to discuss place, direction and distance in this chapter. All of these are difficult to estimate, but part of the fun of learning how to do horary charts is to test your skills in this area. First we'll explore place and direction, and then we will go on to see how we do at determining distance — meaning how far you will move, or how far away is the object, or whatever. These are challenges for all astrologers!

Place and Direction

Horary astrology has special rules for finding out where something is. The determination of place, direction and distance is even less infallible, however, than the determination of time. Although the rules are clear enough here, too, we stand in even greater need of ingenuity in applying them.

The signs and houses give straightforward indications of the compass points as follows:

Stars

• The four cardinal signs give the four cardinal points: Aries is East, Cancer is North, Libra is West and Capricorn is South.

• The other two signs of an element contain the compass point of the cardinal sign as a component. Thus all fire signs indicate an easterly direction.

• The cardinal signs give direction in its purest form — thus Aries is due East. The fixed and mutable signs have as their second component one of two neighboring cardinal points. The diametrically opposite cardinal point may not be used. In other words, there is no such direction as "easterly-westerly," for example.

• The fixed sign of an element always has a northerly or easterly component; the mutable has a southerly or westerly component. Thus, Leo is a fire sign with East as its cardinal direction. But Leo is somewhat to the north of exact East. On the other hand, Sagittarius represents somewhere easterly but toward the south of due East. It is not easy to tell where the sign sectors coalesce.

Taken together, these rules present us with the information shown in Table 6. The houses, too, can be assigned to the points of the compass.

However, if we identify these points on a compass card (the black dots show which ones are used), we find that they appear to have been

Table 6. Directions of the Signs and Houses.

Sign	Direction	House	Direction
Aries	East	1	East
Leo	North of East	2	North by East
Sagittarius	South of East	3	Northeast
Cancer	North	4	North
Scorpio	East of North	5	North by West
Pisces	West of North	6	West-Northwest
Libra	West	7	West
Aquarius	North of West	8	West by South
Gemini	South of West	9	Southwest
Capricorn	South	10	South
Taurus	East of South	11	Southeast by East
Virgo	West of South	12	East-Southeast

chosen at random. Thus there is an angle of one point between North and North by East (11 = ¹/₄°), a three-point angle between North by East and Northeast (33 = ³/₄°), and four points between Northeast and East (45°). And the partitioning varies from quadrant to quadrant. (See figure 6.)

Now, although it seems inevitable that the efficiency of time and direction determination must depend to some degree on personal intuition and choice, it is perfectly possible that a more tidily arranged compass card would yield just as good, if not better, results. Such a rearrangement is illustrated in fig. 7 (p. 112). Because the house sizes (on average 30°) and the spacing between the points (22–¹/₂°) do not coincide, we must make do with roughly estimated sectors.

In each case, the houses follow the points around the compass card but the signs do not. Whereas Pisces gives a direction West of

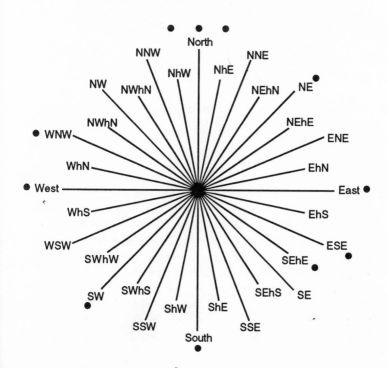

Figure 6. Compass points.

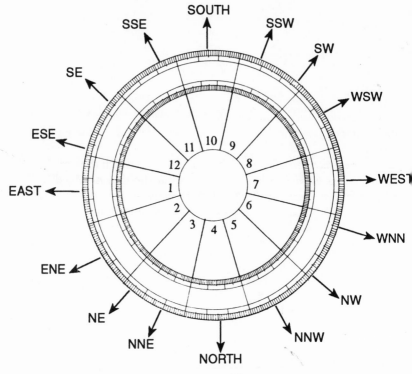

Figure 7. A more modern compass guide.

North, the corresponding 12th house gives East-southeast. But, in any case, the signs and houses are used separately although there is no unanimity as to their use. Some people find a meaning by combining the sign and house in which the significator stands. If that creates difficulties, they take the Moon as co-significator and let its sign and house decide the direction. In practice, this can involve a lot of juggling and weighing one thing against another. To return to the examples given above, say Pisces is in the 12th house, then we are faced with the problem of finding some way of combining West of North (say North-northwest) with East-southeast — an impossible task.

Now suppose that, in addition, the Moon is in Libra in 7. This adds two more westerly indications, which could be interpreted as tipping the scales in favor of West. But this method is not particularly straightforward. We have to rely on our intuition quite a lot!

Another method is to take the sign on the cusp of the house of the quesited as a guide to the main direction, and the sign and house in which the significator of the quesited stands as guides to subsidiary locations. Then, once we have come to the place suggested by the main direction, we can fan out in these subsidiary directions. I have had a certain amount of success with this method, although it is certainly not foolproof.

Some other practitioners look at the house in which the significator is posited for the main direction, and at the sign in which it is posited for a subsidiary direction. If we revert to the Pisces/12th house example, we find that the house indicates East-southeast—the main direction—and Pisces indicates West of North. Therefore the main direction is pulled more to the East; *or*, once we are in the room or area lying in the main direction, we need to continue our search in the northwestern part.

There is no harm in trying all the methods. Although I, myself, have had good results with the second method on many occasions, the last method also seems to bear fruit at times. Clear pointers to interpretation though there may be, this part of horary astrology is still in the experimental stage.

A further method, which also seems to work in practice, is the following: determine the significator of the quesited and note the sign and house it occupies. Take the element to which the sign belongs as a rough guide to the direction, and take the house as an indication of relative distance. The distances are not absolute of course. They are determined like this:

• *Cardinal houses* (1, 4, 7, 10) show that the quesited is very near at hand. For instance, a lost object would be somewhere in the house, or where we generally employ it, or where it belongs (a file at the office, etc.).

• *Succedent houses* (2, 5, 8, 11) show that the article is not in the house or in the place where it is generally employed. But it is fairly close at hand. If the article is a pan that has gone missing from the kitchen, it will be in the garage, the garden, or so on.

• *Cadent houses* (3, 6, 9, 12) are the most difficult indications, because they concern places that are far away, out of reach, or concealed. There is a danger that the lost object will not be recovered, or the goal not obtained. The 3rd house forms something of an exception because it has to do with short distances; but it can still present problems.

The quickness with which the quesited will be found may also be read from the houses. If the significator is in a cardinal house, the missing object or the quesited will be found soon without too much searching. In succedent houses we have to expend more effort and the object is harder to find; while in cadent houses we shall never find what we are looking for, however hard we try. It is still possible, even in cadent houses, that the object may turn up by accident or in some other indirect manner.

In order to discover whether or not something (or someone) will be found, we need to observe the basic rules. In other words, first look to see if the significators of the querent and the quesited make — or are in the process of making — positive contact. This will reveal if the lost thing or person will turn up again. If, in such a situation, the significator of the quesited is in a cadent house, we can say that the lost item or the quesited will come into the possession of the querent (again), but in an indirect manner, by accident or by chance, unexpectedly and not through any effort of the querent.

The significator of the lost item, even in an angle, does not promise the return of the item without more ado, we would hasten to add. Before that is assumed, we must see if the significators of the querent and the quesited are in positive contact. If so, the angular house can indicate that this positive answer will soon become reality — more quickly than the time prediction shows. Using this method, the elements indicate the following locations:

Fire signs (Aries, Leo, Sagittarius): middle floor and ceiling, or middle height. In a house, the upper, but not the top, stories. The east side of a room, house, etc. Places to do with fire or iron — chimney, stove, open hearth, the place where the heater stands, and so on.

Earth signs (Taurus, Virgo, Capricorn): floor level in the room, or on the ground floor of a house or building. On the pavement, in the cellar, or on the ground, the gravel path or tiled path round the house. The south side of a room, a wall, etc.

Air signs (Gemini, Libra, Aquarius): the highest story of a house, the highest part of a room, the roof and the eaves, the highest storage space in the room or house (the highest shelf in the corner cupboard, for instance). The western side of anything.

Water signs (Cancer, Scorpio, Pisces): low-lying parts of the house or of a room, especially where there is water; thus near the sink, in the bathroom, by the water pipes. Outside, in the vicinity of the rainpipe, pond, or swimming pool. The northern side of anything.

To this, it should be added that, when the significator is on or close to the cusp of a house, it enters new terrain (a new house) so to speak. Naturally, one then thinks of an entrance or exit; and in fact it often happens in such a case that the missing item is near a door, a window, a gate, a boundary post, or a fence dividing two pieces of land.

In addition, each sign has a number of places that specifically belong to it, so that we can further refine the indications obtained from the elements if we are still in doubt. We can, with a little imagination, deduce for ourselves the places in question, with the help of what has already been said and with the help of our knowledge of the signs. Thus, all air and fire signs have to do with more elevated positions, and so on. The list that follows provides a number of examples of places belonging to the different signs. Some places can come under several signs. Which one we choose depends on the most prominent characteristic of the matter in hand.

ARIES: Territory that has only just been opened up, freshly tilled or plowed land, virgin soil that is ready to be reclaimed, sandy or hilly ground. Areas scorched by the sun or by fire. Areas occupied by pioneers and other free spirits, e.g., beaches reserved for nudists.

Shops or workshops where (sharp) tools are employed, such as garages, forges, barbershops, dental surgeries, hardware stores and the like. Things and workshops in which heat plays a part also come under Aries, e.g., blast-furnaces. Then there are places where cutting is done—the butcher's shop and the operating theater (the latter can come under Scorpio). The ovens in a bakery come under Aries, but the flour and bread come under Cancer and Virgo.

In the home, Aries governs the open fire, the stove, the oven, the cooker or range, and the central heating boiler—also the watchdog's kennel, the top-story ceiling, the eastern part of the rooms in the house, and so on.

TAURUS: Gardens, especially well-kept gardens around the house, lawns, bushes, and trees by the house, cattle sheds, and farms. The offices of brokers and bankers, vaults, safe deposit boxes, and other places where valuables are stored, such as a locked private room. Places where expensive items are stored or where money is earned from their sale.

In the home, Taurus governs storage spaces, quiet rooms, rooms with soft lighting, rooms with low ceilings, basements, cellars. The southeast side of rooms, walls, or houses.

GEMINI: In the landscape, hilly or high-lying areas, usually within walking distance, but the path is climbing. In urban areas, the places where the road signs are, the streets, traffic lights and billboards.

Places where information plays a part—libraries, presses, book shops, studies, schools, and colleges. Also places to do with the processing and transmission of information—shops selling stationery, offices, telephones and their exchanges. Connecting links, such as post boxes and offices, trains, buses, ships, cars, bicycles, parking places, the railroad station, the airport, the garage, etc.

In the home, Gemini governs the study, the place where the telephone stands, the stairs and the doors (which connect the different parts of the house!), the upstairs rooms, the highest part of the room or of the house, the upper part of the bookcase, the tops of the various pieces of furniture, and so on. the lofts of stables and outbuildings. The west-southwest side of rooms, houses and gardens.

CANCER: Places containing water, close to water or having to do with water in some way—such as fountains, lakes, canals, rivers, springs, aqueducts, reservoirs; also the shores of lakes, coastal areas, the banks of rivers and the like. Offices of institutions mainly concerned with water supply and food control, such as waterworks, water boards, food inspection departments, plumbers and their subcontractors.

In the home, Cancer governs everything to do with water, such as the bathroom, the shower, the sink, the laundry room, the pump or faucet. Also anything to do with food—the kitchen cupboard, the vegetable bin, the dining room. The north side of anywhere.

LEO: Places with a chic or decorative function. Places where children play, such as playrooms, playgrounds and the like. Also, places mainly concerned with amusement and recreation, such as parks, zoological gardens, theaters, casinos, cinemas, and so on.

As a fire sign, Leo, where the countryside is concerned, has to do with fairly high, rocky areas. Fire comes in a recreational way — the place round the barbecue for instance. Leo also represents protected areas where wild animals live, such as nature reserves, national parks, woods and primeval forests.

In the home, Leo governs the nursery, the playroom, the recreation room, the hobby room, the sitting-room, the place where cards are played. Also the place where there is fire, such as the fireplace and the oven (but these come under other signs as well). Sometimes Leo refers to an (at the time) untidy room. The east-northeast side of anything.

VIRGO: Flat, fertile farmland, cornfields, (kitchen) gardens, meadows, cultivated land, animal sheds, storage space for crops, and enterprises making diary products. Also: cold stores, barns, silos and the like, and the concerns that have to do with them.

In the home, Virgo governs places for storing food, mainly for food that has to be kept for a fairly long time. The freezer, the place where animal feed is stored, but also the medicine cabinet and the sick-room. Also under Virgo come the room where we do our domestic accounts, etc. The study can also come here. Also bookcases, offices (which thus come under several signs), and so on. Sometimes a rented room comes under Virgo. The south-southwest side of anything.

LIBRA: Areas blessed with clear, pure air, mountain meadows, hills and especially the tops of these, detached buildings (often on uncultivated land or on stony ground or gravel).

Airy places such as verandas, or light rooms, or the highest rooms, the attic. Places where clothes and luxury items are kept; also shops and other outlets for ornaments and works of art, clothing and luxury services. Places where people meet socially.

In the home, Libra governs the bedroom, the dressing-room, the room where pictures and/or ornaments are displayed, the cloakroom and wardrobe, and the higher parts of the rooms and of the house. The western part of anything.

SCORPIO: Marshy and swampy areas, stagnant pools, places infested with rodents, snakes, worms, reptiles and the like. Places where rotting processes take place, or where trash is thrown.

Enterprises concerned with the handling of waste, oil, gas and their (breakdown!) products, with sewers and sewer-laying. Lavatories and cesspools also come under Scorpio.

Graveyards, crematoria, and morticians' parlors belong to Scorpio. Although the ordinary first-aid cabinet normally comes under Virgo, the place where dangerous medicines are stored comes under Scorpio. The storage place is generally locked and hidden. Rooms that cannot be opened—subterranean vaults and the like—are Scorpionic. Ruins are assigned to Capricorn as well as to Scorpio; but, if they are situated in or near water, they belong to Scorpio alone. The north-northeast side of anything.

SAGITTARIUS: Like the other fire signs, Sagittarius has to do with hilly, higher ground that is clearly visible—usually, the sort of ground belonging to Sagittarius is suitable for large buildings. Forests are particularly Sagittarian (also good hunting country). Sacred sites and places of pilgrimage, temples, mosques, churches, monasteries and the like are Sagittarian, too, (although religious institutions can also come under Pisces).

Race courses and dog tracks, bookmakers and stables. Also sports stadiums, and racing circuits for cars. Army barracks and camps; and, according to some, arsenals as well.

Attorneys' offices and educational establishments. University colleges and campuses, and courts of law (although the latter also belongs to Libra). Fire can also come into the picture in the form of places close to fire or heat, such as stoves and the like.

In the home, Sagittarius governs warm places and the spot where a weapon or sporting-gun and the ammunition for it is kept; the big rooms in the house and/or those that are upstairs; also rooms containing a safe, or where several impressive private possessions—such as valuable heirlooms—are deposited. The east-southeast side of anything.

CAPRICORN: Very lonely, out-of-the-way places, wildernesses and depressed areas such as fallow, deserted ground, ghost towns, slums, etc. Mountain peaks, cold and inaccessible mountains, but also mines and mining districts, and areas that supply large quantities of timber for industry. Ruins and graveyards.

Government buildings and buildings for other official bodies, districts where most of a town's commercial life goes on. Together with Scorpio: cemeteries, tax offices and institutions.

Storage places for wood, pit-coal and other minerals, and for agricultural implements.

In the home, Capricorn governs dark, somberly furnished rooms that are poorly lit and never sunny; dark corners in rooms, the cold cellar, places with low ceilings, places close to the ground, places where old, often broken articles are stored. The south side of anything.

AQUARIUS: In the landscape, hilly, uneven ground, which is quite likely to have undergone a change of use; for example, from agricultural land to land for houses or industry. Land that has been reclaimed from nature by the application of technology and ingenuity—e.g., deserts that have been turned into orchards, and the polders of The Netherlands.

All places where modern engineering, inventions, electronics, aeronautics and the like play an important role, such as airfields, television and radio studios, scientific research laboratories and institutions where technical inspections are performed. Also, all places to do with advanced communications and research come under Aquarius.

Aquarian areas are often well to the fore; that is to say, places with good transport facilities. Also, high tension cables, and generating stations, and the technical part of a nuclear reactor. (The raw material, Uranium, comes under Aquarius, but the deadly radiations come under Scorpio.)

In the home, Aquarius governs the higher parts of rooms, the upper stories, the electrical lines, the electric meter, the room(s) where ultra-modern architecture and furnishings are in evidence. The power points, modern labor-saving devices for the kitchen, also the cupboard where the modern electrical implements and kitchen-ware are stored. The west-northwest side of anything.

PISCES: Low-lying land susceptible to flooding, such as the estuary of a river. Coastal regions (together with Cancer), bays, and places where there are springs. Swampy ground. This is clearer and less boggy than the swampy ground assigned to Scorpio. What is more, everything to do with bathing and swimming belongs to Pisces, such as swimming baths, bath houses and the like. Also whatever has to do with fish: fishmongers, fishing boats, fishing grounds, fish restaurants and so on. Very damp places where many parasitic plants thrive.

Hospitals, sanatoria, cleaning companies, chemical factories and gas companies, gas pipes, gasometers, and places where chemicals and cleaning agents are stored.

Places where water and other liquids (drinks) are processed, also intoxicants, and places where poisonous medicines are kept (under lock and key). Kneipp hydros, where the healing power of water is employed, and other places where the healing arts, and especially alternative medicine (e.g., magnetism) are exercised.

Places where illusion, in the widest sense of the word, is used: the tinsel of the theater, photographic studios and shops selling photographic equipment and accessories, film studios (which have so aptly been called dream factories), and so on. The dressing room of a theatrical company generally comes under Pisces, too.

Prisons and prison cells fall under Pisces. In the home, Pisces governs rooms with low ceilings, rooms with cold and/or damp floors, the photographic darkroom. The north-northwest side of a house or room.

Distance

If direction is hard to determine, in spite of the available rules, then distance is even more so. Indeed, the problem is so hard that a number of modern horary specialists have given it up altogether. The estimation of distance is not particularly old, as we can see from the fact that the English mile (= 1609 meters) is used; which would suggest that the practice arose in an English-speaking area. Apart from the awkwardness of a unit of 1609 meters, a question mark hangs over the universal status of this mile. It is very doubtful if we ought to regard it as universally valid. Nevertheless, when combined with the existing rules, this measure can give results, and is therefore worthy of some attention. Because we are generally more interested in approximate rather than precise distances, I myself work with a mile value rounded down to 1500 meters, and this seems to be quite satisfactory in practice.

First let us see what the rules have to say to us. As usual, we take the significator of the quesited or of the missing person or object (nearly always the house ruler), and inquire if the significator has north, south, or zero latitude. The Sun's latitude is always zero, but that of the planets can vary. (Look in the latitude column next to the declinations in the ephemeris.) The significator's house taken with its latitude, gives the basic unit of distance for our calculations. The details are as follows:

Planet in:	Latitude 0	Latitude North	Latitude South
Angular house	close by	± 1.5 km	± 3.0 km
Succedent house	± 0.75 km	± 3.0 km	± 4.5 km
Cadent house	± 1.5 km	± 4.5 km	very far

Now take the degree occupied by the Moon and the degree occupied by the significator and find their difference without considering the difference (if any) between the signs they are in. For example, Moon 12° Libra and significator 23° Leo. Difference: 23° – 12° = 11°. Multiply this difference in degrees by the basic distance found already.

When the Moon is the significator of the missing item (i.e., when Cancer is on the cusp of the house concerned), we take the difference between the degree in which the Moon is posited and the degree on the cusp of the house over which the Moon rules. This method will not always work; but there is a variant which also seems to be effective at times. In this, we look not at the latitude of the significator of the quesited, but at the latitude of the Moon, using the same scheme as before. The rest is precisely the same except that we use the house in which the Moon is posited as our starting point.

Let us examine both methods with the help of Chart 8 from the previous chapter (see page 100). Venus was the significator of our future residence, and Mars was our significator. Venus was in a cadent house. On May 19, 1980, Venus had north latitude, therefore our unit of distance is ± 4.5 km. The difference between Venus and the Moon is 4° 42′ – 2° 04′ = 2° 38′. In decimals, 2° 38′ is 2.63. So we have 2.63 × 4.5 km = 11.84 km approximately (our unit of distance is only a rough reminder). According to this calculation, our new home would be some 12 km from the old home, which does not seem to fit the facts at all well.

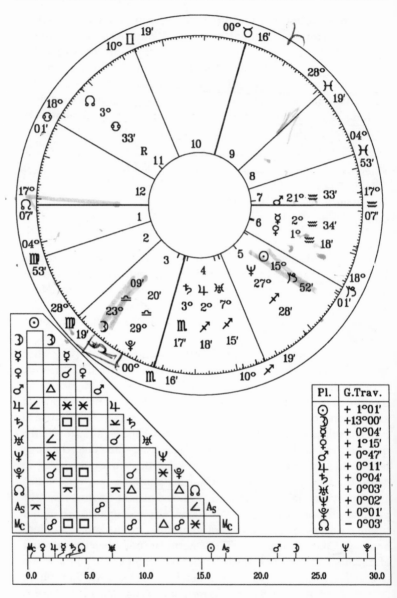

Chart 10. Who called? Amsterdam, Holland (52 N 22, 4 E 54), January 6, 1983, 6:30 P.M. GMT. Placidus houses. Chart calculated by Astrolabe using *Nova Printwheels*.

But if we use the Moon as our indicator of latitude, we get a very different result. The Moon had south latitude on May 19, 1980, which gives a completely different measure. The Moon is in an angle and, since the latitude is south, our unit is 3 km. Now take the difference in degrees between the Moon and Venus, which is 2° 38' or 2.63, and multiply 3 km by this. We then obtain a distance of 7.89 km. In reality, the new house seems to be about 7 km from the old (not as the crow flies, but according to the shortest route between the two houses). Hence this example pleads in favor of the second method, in which the Moon is taken as the starting point. But, be that as it may, we do have to be on our guard when using these rules, as long as the last word has not been said about them.

The following determination of distance is employed mainly for straying animals and missing persons. Where missing possessions are concerned, use is quite often made of the following method: take the Lord of 1 for the querent, and the Lord of 2 for the missing object and find the degree difference between the two, again without bothering about the difference in signs. The sign occupied by the Moon decides the multiplication factor thus:

Moon in a cardinal sign = distance × 2
Moon in a fixed sign   = distance × $1/4$
Moon in a mutable sign   = distance × $1/2$

The distance is reckoned in one English mile per degree, or less accurately in ca. 1 = $1/2$ kilometers per degree.

If the Moon rules both 1 and 2, we take the Moon solely as ruler of 1 and the degree on the 2nd cusp as significator of the missing object; and usually we also apply the rules mentioned previously.

Of course, we can combine distance and direction and, with a little ingenuity, can apply the above rules to other situations. To give an example, one evening I was feeding our newborn baby when the phone rang. I was unable to pick it up but was naturally curious to know who was calling. Therefore I noted the time in order to make a horary chart. See Chart 10.

A phone call belongs to the 3rd house. The significator of the person who rang is Mercury. My significator is the Sun. The caller has several significators that are less important than the ruler of the sign on the 3rd cusp, yet still capable of playing some part: Venus (Libra is completely intercepted), Pluto and the Moon, although the Moon is also my cosignificator. None of the caller's significators makes contact with my significator; this tallies with the fact that I did not pick up the phone.

But how do we go about discovering who the caller was; or, at least, where the call originated? I took the ruler of 1 and the ruler of 3 and found the difference between the two in terms of degrees. The difference between the Sun and Mercury is 15° 52′ – 2° 34′ = 13° 18′. This difference has to be multiplied by a basic figure; and here I was faced with the problem of deciding what that was. Should I take the latitude of the Moon or the latitude of Mercury, or should I use some other method? Since I had not always had very much success with latitudes, I chose the other rule I have given you. This tells us that when the Moon is in a cardinal sign, we must multiply by two. The Moon is in the cardinal sign Libra here, so I took 2 × 13° 18′, which in decimals is 26.6. We multiply this again by 1.5 km to get 39.9 km. Of course, this is only an approximation, not an exact number of kilometers. The inference was that I had to look for the caller at a distance of around 40 km from my home.

There was still the direction to determine. One method I have found quite satisfactory is that in which the sign on the cusp of the house concerned shows the main direction, and the placement of the ruler of that house shows a second direction that refines the first. Cusp 3 is Virgo, giving a direction West of South. Mercury is in Aquarius in 6. Aquarius gives North of West, and the 6th house (a confirmatory) West-northwest. I decided to see if there was a likely place in the sector between Southwest and South-southwest of Amsterdam. In this place, I had then to look for somewhere in a direction between Northwest and West-northwest. The following day, I discovered who had rung: a friend living in Zoetermeer (about 216° or Southwest to South of our house), approximately 40 km from Amsterdam. He stated that he lived in the Northwest of this place.

Unfortunately, we do not always score such direct hits. Sometimes we shall be very wide of the mark. There are no hard-and-fast rules I can give you, but by experimenting and by combining the various methods you will gradually get results.

Another drawback of the above mentioned method is that we can get no further than a certain distance. For there is no greater degree difference obtainable between the significator and the Moon than nearly 30°, and the greatest multiplication factor is 4.5 km, so that the greatest distance is some 130 km; after which we go off into "infinity."

Experiments with more distant places have unfortunately not given results from which any regular rules can be derived.

For one final example, let us turn back again to Chart 8 (page 100). We can now ask the question where the new house is situated or, in other words, in what part of the city it lies. Its significator, Venus, is in Cancer, in the 9th house; but the cusp of the house representing our new home is Libra. If we look to Libra for the main direction and to the house position of the significator for supplementary information, we find that Libra gives us a Westerly direction and the 9th house a South-southwesterly direction. In fact, our new home was to the west of our old home, and it was south-southwest from the center of Amsterdam. The sign Cancer (North), occupied by Venus, appears to play no part in the determination of the direction.

9

Horary Charts
in Relationship
to Natal Charts

After casting the horary chart as usual, the planets and house cusps of the querent's natal chart can be placed just inside the rim; and then we can use them to provide supplementary information. This interpretative device is known as the Adjusted Horary Chart. Although there are few hard-and-fast rules for dealing with the adjusted horary chart, much can be done by an imaginative application of basic astrological knowledge. Here are a few of the possibilities:

See if a radical planet falls in the 1st house of the horary chart. A radical planet rising in a horary chart often gives additional information on the problems confronting the querent. It can tip the scales one way or the other when different indications are evenly balanced.

Radical planets in other houses of the horary chart can also be used in our interpretation. We apply the nature of the planet concerned in the following way. Say our radical Uranus falls in the 10th house; this can be a further sign that far-reaching, sudden changes are about to take place in 10th house matters; for example, in the querent's social and/or professional position.

Another step we can take is to treat the radical planets as if they were radical houses when interpreting the horary chart. Suppose

Uranus is Lord of 9 in the radix and falls in the 1st house of the horary chart; this can point to the fact that we are actively engaged in study or travel, or shall be shortly. If the horary chart itself does *not* point in the same direction as the radical planet or ruler, there is little the latter can do; but, if it does, then radical positions in the horary chart will enormously strengthen the tendency shown.

Naturally, we can also look at aspects between horary and radical planets. If we think about it for a moment, we shall realize that the horary chart is a form of transit over our birth chart, and on this count alone may be expected to give us information on the course of events. My own experience teaches that it is wrong to limit ourselves to transits, and that we can safely use the other progressions, such as primary and secondary progressions, too. If we are prepared to be thorough, we can take all the progressions in our horoscope. In practice, however, horary questions are seldom so far-reaching that they cannot be answered without the progressions of the querent's birth chart. Generally speaking, we shall find all we need in the horary chart; although not supplemented with radical planets and points.

Thus, we can combine the birth chart with the horary chart. This will not nullify conflicting tendencies in the horary chart, but will soften them.

Changes often take place in the areas represented by those horary chart houses in which the radical Moon, radical Saturn and radical Uranus fall. Where the radical Sun, radical Venus or radical Jupiter fall, we often find some sort of improvement or help, but Saturn tends to bring care, anxiety, or restrictions. The house where we encounter radical Saturn is often the house that keeps us very busy and therefore carries considerable weight in the horary chart. Extra weight can also be carried by the house where we find radical Mercury in the horary chart: this shows what occupies the querent's thoughts.

Radical Mars can have a convulsive and turbulent effect, but it can also have to do with operations and the like. If the question is about a health matter and radical Mars is in horary 1, 6, 8, or 12, then it is very possible that an operation will be considered.

Radical Neptune tends to make matters indistinct and chaotic in the horary house it occupies, and usually creates a certain amount of confusion. Radical Pluto is difficult to interpret. Its effect is often unperceived because it has a lot to do with what is hidden and repressed. But, if the rest of the chart concurs, Pluto can locate the "time bomb" for us, the point where the power struggle breaks out, or the issue that is going to force a confrontation. Frequently Pluto seems to be telling us nothing, and it is not till later that we see what it was doing.

There is still another method by which we can let the radix add a word or two to the interpretation. Place the radical planets along the outer edge of the horary chart and look, not at what radical houses they rule, but at the houses they would rule in the horary chart. If, for example, Venus rules houses 2 and 9 in the radix, it can rule houses 5, 6, and 10 in the horary chart because of the different house distribution. What we do is to treat radical Venus in the horary house as ruler of the horary houses that come under Venus. In fact, we then have in the horary chart, two rulers of 5, two rulers of 6, and two rulers of 10, namely Horary Venus, the natural ruler, and Venus as the radical ruler. In practice, allowance can be made for this without too much trouble; always bearing in mind that this factor cannot alter the basic interpretation of the horary chart, any more than a good horary chart can cancel a difficult constellation in our radix—although it can alleviate its effect.

When Things Happen

In daily life it is not always easy to explain why an event occurred at a given moment or why we did something when we did. There is only one way to find out, and that is to cast a horary for the moment when such things happen to see what can be learned from them. In my opinion, because we tend to ignore the astrological significance of familiar, regularly occurring events, we let a lot of useful information slip through our fingers. For, in fact, the connection between the birth chart and the moment when everyday events happen seems to be very important.

What is immediately obvious, when we study such events, is that at least one of the four cardinal points of the horary chart (Ascendant, Descendant, MC, and IC), appears, in the majority of cases, to be conjunct a radical planet or cusp, or to be making a major aspect to a radical planet or cusp. I could give whole rows of examples, but one or two will be enough to illustrate what I mean.

Our car had three blow-outs within a period of three months. Such a thing had never happened to us before, nor has it happened since. The fact that the blow-outs occurred within such a short space of time could be explained by the progressions for my husband and myself; but the moment when they happened was remarkable. The first blow-out was at front right, where I always sit. The horary chart for that moment had an Ascendant that fell exactly on my radical Uranus! No planet is more appropriate for a blow-out than Uranus. The second blow-out was also on the front right of the car. Now the MC of the horary chart stood exactly on my radical Uranus; the orb in both cases was less than one degree. The third blow-out was at front left, in front of the driving seat where my husband always sits. "That has to be my Uranus," he sighed. The MC of the horary chart was at 18° Gemini, his Uranus exactly!

To give another example, I had promised a friend to phone her on Sunday. But however hard I tried, she did not answer. Later in the day, I tried again, this time with success. She insisted that she had been in all day. The horary chart for my first attempt had an Ascendant that fell right on her radical Neptune, almost exactly within a minute of arc. That telephone call obviously got lost in the typical Neptunian mist.

I have seen the exactness of a horary cusp on a radical point time after time. I had an appointment with my general practitioner and arrived at his office in good time. But there was no one there to see me. I decided to wait and, in the meantime, several other patients who had appointments arrived. It seems that the doctor had been called out to an accident. Not till very much later did he return to resume his practice, and even then he made a number of phone calls first. The moment I stepped into his consulting room, the Ascendant of the horary chart fell exactly on my radical Moon.

Something very similar happened on my visit to a new dentist. As I entered the waiting room in time for my appointment, the MC was making an exact square to my radical Venus, the ruler of my 2nd house. "This is going to cost me!" was the thought that flashed through my mind; a thought that turned out to be all too true. I was kept waiting a long time. When my turn finally came, the horary MC was conjunct my radical Saturn, the ruler of bones, hair, and teeth. The conjunction was exact and, of course, very appropriate. It looks as if I had had to wait until one of the moving points of the horary chart was activated.

To prepare a chart for every minor event would be an almost impossible task. Therefore it is useful to make ourselves a set of mini house tables for the degree of latitude where we live. Better still are the various disks of house data from which we can immediately take a fairly accurate reading of the house cusps after a glance at the clock. If we want to work very quickly, then an astrowatch, an astrological watch that shows the actual MC and the actual ascendant is a great help for we can see the astrological significance of these minor events whenever we wish.[1]

This form of instant horary astrology can be very enlightening, because it can give us an insight into the wheels within wheels of astrology; also we can tune in to what is going on more quickly than we would otherwise do. For instance, I have memorized the birth charts of many of my relatives and friends. When the house phone rings, I quite often hazard a successful guess at who is on the other end of the line. In many cases, one of the four cardinal points of the horary chart aspects a personal point in the horoscope of the person making the call. And often the planet concerned reveals the subject of the conversation and the motive behind it.

Frequently one encounters someone just as an important planet or angle is being activated by the Ascendant or Midheaven of the horary chart. If we suddenly think of a person then, ten to one, his or her Sun or Moon or other important horoscope factor is being aspected by the current ASC or MC.

I have a growing conviction that astrology affects the most minute details in life. It is curious how we start thinking of someone when a point is being aspected in his or her chart; or unexpectedly decide on some course of action that is in keeping with the position of the ASC or MC at the moment. Thus, for a week, my husband had been begging me to cut his hair. But I know that, once I start on him, I do not let him go until I am satisfied with the result, and it is not always that I feel like making the effort. I kept putting it off until, suddenly, I rose from the typewriter. I was up to my eyes in work, preparing a

---

[1] In Europe we have plastic pocket disks with movable parts which enable you to find the exact positions of the house cusps for any day and time you want at a certain degree and latitude. We can get them for 46°, 48°, 50°, 52° or 54°, so if you are on holiday in Europe, you can make instant horary charts. They are only made for the first 20 degrees east of Greenwich. The astro-watch is a pocketwatch with a special disk that allows you to immediately see the midheaven and ascendant of the moment. I use both of these items, and they may at some point be available in the USA, although I understand that people are able to do instant charts on their computers today and can quickly answer horary questions as so many computers are portable now.

lecture, but I called him to come to me. "Bring me the scissors," I said, "If you like I'll cut your hair now!" I was quite surprised at the sudden urge that rose up in me to give him his trim at last, but even more surprised when I saw that the MC for that moment stood exactly on my husband's radical Saturn, that is to say on the planet of bones, teeth, and hair! Does my unconscious mind know how to read my husband's body clock? It would seem so, for why else should I have been prompted to make his hair tidy at such an appropriate moment?

Because I lead a very busy life, and tend to have too many irons in the fire, there are times when I feel positively fatigued. More often than not, these lows in the day occur when the MC or the ASC are in conjunction or are making a hard aspect to my radical Saturn. Examples could be piled up endlessly, but what they all amount to is this: it seems clear that things happen at their own special moments, and these moments are closely dependent on the individual.

The angles of the corresponding horary charts may always be expected to be in some sort of aspect with points in the radix. Astrology seems to be in tune with quite minor circumstances. Everyone has their own astrological rhythm, which can be studied in the movement of the ASC and MC through the zodiac.

Things happen when the time is ripe. The Ascendant and Midheaven aspect all points in the radix during twenty-four hours. Nevertheless, different things happen each day. Therefore we need to state the case rather guardedly, like this: if something is ready to happen, it generally happens at a suitable moment. But if nothing is ready to happen, nothing is activated and there is nothing to observe when the otherwise suitable moment arrives. Thus I do not feel tired every day when my Saturn is aspected, but if I have been under pressure, I feel the aspecting of Saturn very strongly. So it makes sense to study one's own progressions in order to see which points are receiving the emphasis in a certain period and are most likely to influence us during the daily progress of the Midheaven and Ascendant.

The connection between the birth chart and the horary chart is therefore more significant than we think. For example, I once had a phone call informing me that I was going to be invited to cooperate on a long-term project. The horary chart of the phone call was positive and indicated that I ought to accept the invitation. However, the call came at a moment when the Ascendant stood exactly on my radical Saturn. I did indeed set to work on the project, and with pleasure too, but jobs kept coming in when it was not convenient, at times when I did not fancy them, or was feeling weary, or had other important things to do. In short, my radical Saturn was constantly interfering; and this is something that was not obvious from the horary chart alone, but could be anticipated only by combining the horary chart and the radix.

The Horary Chart as a Means of Rectifying the Radix

As soon as it dawned on me that important factors in the radix are activated at the moments when various daily events occur: especially the radical Sun, Moon, Mercury, Ascendant and Midheaven, I decided to find out the extent to which horary charts could help in the rectification of birth charts. I rather expected that I would keep encountering a radical Ascendant or MC, although I naturally looked out for other radical points. I made up my mind just to let things come to me, leaving the initiative to those whose horoscopes needed to be rectified. Almost immediately I was presented with a golden opportunity. A foreigner who occasionally visited The Netherlands came into the place where I was working at the time. He was interested in astrology and wanted to have his horoscope cast, but did not know his exact time of birth. His mother had told him that he was born between a quarter past eleven and twelve o'clock at night, but that was all. I asked him for important events in his life so that I could carry out a rectification, but he could not think of any. Owing to an accident, he was suffering from a loss of memory and could recollect nothing more than vague impressions and feelings; he could not recall specific events, let alone the dates on which the latter had taken place. Naturally, this was a very complicated case. I thought I would just consider the Ascendant and the Midheaven for the moment he entered the place of business, to see if these would provide any clues, especially as he used to come back there several times a year.

The first time he returned, the Ascendant was 17° Libra. A few months later he came again, and the MC was 17° Libra. After that, we heard no more of him for a while until, suddenly, he walked in through the door and, guess what, 17° Libra was on the Ascendant! I then thought I had something to go on, so I looked for a time between quarter past eleven and twelve o'clock at night when an MC, IC,

Ascendant or Descendant was at 17° Libra. For a time of 11:38 P.M. (23:38 h.), I obtained an Ascendant of 17° Libra—a direct hit. To make assurance doubly sure, I went through the progressions for the current year with him, to see whether what was shown by the progressions corresponded with reality. To our amazement and delight, the results were first class.

A very similar case was presented to me not long afterward. I had a phone call from a good friend who asked me if I would cast a horoscope for a foreign friend of his, a concert guitarist who was in difficulties. But his time of birth was unknown, and he asked if that would be a problem. I immediately made a note of the moment when the friend's horoscope was mentioned. My answer to the question was that it was virtually impossible to overcome the lack of a birth-time, but I was willing to do what I could. I wrote down the time and place of birth and assumed that the man must have been born at some time between midnight and sunrise. The uncertainty over his time of birth was due to the fact that the midwife thought he was stillborn, and it was several hours before it was discovered that he had a spark of life in him.

I asked for a number of rectification dates from the man's life, and waited for them to be phoned through to me. I did not suggest any time when it would be best to ring me up, for I wanted to leave everything to happen at the right moment. The second phone call came a day later. The MC now stood on the degree where the Ascendant had stood the previous day: 24° Virgo. Several more phone calls followed, in which 24° Virgo continued to figure, and this strengthened my conviction that I was on the right track. I looked to see whether 24° Virgo was on an angle, preferably the ASC or MC, within the time limits I had set. One-and-a-half hours after midnight, 24° Virgo was on the MC, and I felt sure that this would be an acceptable starting point for attempting the rectification. The man had been married a number of times (always fine rectification data . . .) and had had an accident. The dates and the progressions agreed perfectly, so this was the horoscope I took.

The following weekend, the man himself was coming to see me, and our friend and his wife were also coming to do some interpreting if necessary. We had arranged to begin at ten o'clock in the morning, and although our friends were there, the man had not arrived. I looked at my astrological watch and saw that in 32 minutes the MC would be at 24° Virgo; so I said to our friends: "He will come at

10:32." At precisely two minutes after half past, the bell rang and the man stepped through the door!

Here is yet another example of the right moment. As I have already said, I am often under pressure, and I like to work as efficiently as possible. Therefore I use any short quiet periods to calculate and cast horoscopes. On one of the many occasions when I had half an hour to spare, I drew a commissioned birth chart on the computer. As usual, I looked at my astrological timepiece and saw that 8° Scorpio was on the Ascendant. To my amazement, at that very moment 8° Scorpio on the Ascendant flashed onto the screen of the computer. And now, as I sit writing this, 8° Scorpio stands on the Descendant.

Of course, there are other cases that are not so straightforward. As mentioned above, it is not always the Ascendant or the Midheaven that is activated. What is more, the horary Ascendant and Midheaven can fall on personal planets, and this can make the rectification possibilities less clear-cut. I have even noticed that the horary Ascendant and Midheaven (or Descendant and IC) are capable of falling on progressed horoscope positions and so emphasize these, especially the positions of primary and secondary progressions. (See the horary chart of the moment when the woman phoned in the chapter on the consultation horoscope, page 144. The IC of this chart was in the same degree as her progressed Ascendant.) The conclusion is that we can certainly try to rectify by means of horary charts, but we must always be on our guard. Also, rectification with the help of horary charts is very time-consuming. A sufficient number of contact moments is always required for the choice of a specific, constantly recurring degree.

The Nature of the Sign on the MC and Change of Sign

Has it ever struck you that sometimes there suddenly seem to be more people on the street than at other times? And have you ever had the annoying experience of having to wait an unconscionably long time in a line at the post office or supermarket? Next time, take a look at the horary chart of these moments. It is a safe bet that at the moment when everywhere there is a buzz of activity and more people seem to be on the move than usual, the MC (and rather less often the Ascendant) is at the point of changing signs. A sudden rush of people coincides surprisingly often with a change of sign; which takes place approximately once every two hours where the MC is concerned.

The transition involved in a change of sign is not smooth; but, on the contrary, is often very abrupt. It is as if a sharp dividing line ran between the two signs. Here again, numerous examples could be given, but the reader would do well to take the trouble to look for others.

You are hard at work, when suddenly there is an interruption and you decide to take a break. In many cases there is a change of sign at the same time. Or you suddenly lose interest in what you are doing and make up your mind to go and do something else. Here again, we often see that the MC changes from one sign to the next. And more convincingly still, the sign on the MC frequently shows the type of the activity or the meaning the activity has for us. But of this more by-and-by.

We are going on vacation. We stow the baggage in the car, make the final arrangements and then as, sooner or later than planned, we get in to set off, there often seems to be . . . a change of sign.

As we have already seen, the same is true in the post office or at the supermarket. With a change of sign, it is evident that more people have decided to go shopping, and the result is that they get in one another's way. For my part, as soon as I think about going out to fetch something, I first look to see whether there is a change of sign: this saves me from all sorts of delays. But a young acquaintance of mine regularly has the following experience. Her Moon is at exactly 0° of a sign and, if she is standing in a line during a change of sign, an extra counter or check-out point is suddenly opened so that she can take her turn quickly. No wonder: her Moon always makes it "her time." So, in general, activities increase especially at moments when the MC or ASC are activating radical points, or during a change of sign.

In many instances, the sign on the MC sets the tone of the next two hours. I have often observed that the subjects of conversation are in keeping with the sign on the MC. With this in mind, it is very amusing to see what happens during astrological congresses when lectures are being delivered. Thus one speaker began his talk in Taurus. It was quiet, well-constructed, but rather tedious. The room was quiet, too. Then Gemini came on the MC; people started getting restless, and there was a lot of whispering. The busy hum of Gemini was unmistakable. When the man stopped speaking (incidentally, shortly after the change of sign), he received a deluge of questions—another characteristic of Gemini.

Another astrologer rose to speak when Libra was on the MC. His subject was the ethics of astrology—very suitable for such a sign as Libra. After a while, he paused, and looking intently at the audience said, "This seems like a good time to share with you the provisional results of my research into death and the horoscope." At that moment, the MC had just entered Scorpio. The astrologer himself had no idea that 0° Scorpio was on the MC, yet his timing was faultless for introducing this new topic.

The nature of the sign on the MC also interacts with our own birth chart. It appears that, when we take something important in hand, with the MC in a sign that does not fit in with our horoscope or our character, matters turn out to be harder and more awkward than we expect. Therefore, if we have an important interview, we should try to arrange for it to take place during a period when the sign on the MC blends well with our own horoscope.

In connection with the change of sign phenomenon, there is one more thing I wish to point out. The last degrees of a sign, seem often to go with a loss of energy, reduced concentration, and so on. Something new is in the air (the new sign), but it has not yet materialized. The last degrees (sometimes jokingly referred to as "third degrees") are therefore degrees in which plans generally get no further than the drawing board, jobs are not completed, and so on. So it is not surprising that the last degrees of a sign on the Ascendant should warn us against trying to judge the question. That is confirmed in practice. Nevertheless, things do in fact happen when there is some connection with the birth chart, and this creates an exception to the rule about when it is not safe to judge the question, as we have seen.

The Interconnection of Horary Charts

I have sometimes observed that the horary charts of different events apparently overlap one another and the horoscopes of those involved, as the following example illustrates. One evening I received a phone call from the organizer of an annual congress, inviting me to deliver a lecture. The MC had just entered Aquarius—quite an appropriate sign; and it later transpired that the organizer's Mercury was in the same zodiac position. I agreed to speak, but heard nothing further for several months; until the Sun entered Aquarius and reached the MC of the horary chart. Then the organizer rang again. The MC was now at 17° Aries. On the day of the lecture, the Sun was also at 17° Aries. Thus a horary chart is sensitive to transits, and one horary chart can be remarkably interwoven with another.

Furthermore, I have found that progressions and transits in horary charts are often paralleled by progressions and transits in my own radix. We had an automobile accident one unlucky moment — someone in another car collided with us — and a nasty eye injury was the result. Both in my husband's horoscope and in my own, there are indications that could point to an accident or minor accident; among other things, there are conflicts involving the 3rd house (the accident occurred where we were living). But when I cast the horary chart of the purchase of the car, and worked out the secondary progressions, I saw to my amazement an exact square between the Moon and Pluto for the time of the accident; a very apt indication which paralleled our own progressions. The accident happened with the horary MC conjunct my radical Mercury (my ruler of 3, and thus of traffic and short journeys in the place where we live!). The Ascendant of the horary chart of the accident also seems significant. When the Sun was exactly conjunct this Ascendant, the after-effects were over· the car was repaired, the insurance claims had been settled. On the day of the solar transit, we received the final letter from the insurance company advising us of the completion of the matter.

When I later studied the horoscope of our marriage (the moment when the words "I do" were spoken), the warning of an accident seemed to be contained in that, too. All kinds of events, from small to great, therefore appear to be connected by a common thread, both with one another and with the person they affect. By tracing that common thread with the help of horary astrology, we can obtain many new insights.

10

The
Consultation
Horoscope

A horary chart that is suitable for use in the interpretation of progressions for family, friends, acquaintances and clients, is the so-called consultation horoscope. This is the horoscope of the moment at which one of these individuals comes in for a horoscope reading. Time and again, I have found that the situation of this individual is strikingly shown by the chart of the moment he or she arrives.

Over a period of several years, I experimented as follows. Whenever a client rang to make an appointment, I noted the date and time of the conversation next to the birth data of the client. This I used to cast a horary chart, *and* I made a chart for the time of the consultation, the actual moment the client walked in through the door and the moment when we began the interpretation. This makes four charts in all.

People do not always arrive on time. One is ten minutes early, another is seven minutes late. Perhaps the first forgot the precise time of the appointment, and the second had missed the bus or train or got caught in a traffic jam. In other words, there are big variations possible in when a person will actually arrive. (Luckily, most people are no more than ten minutes early or late.) After the client has come in, we often chat over a cup of tea before making a start: another new horoscope. What I wanted to know was which of the four charts would provide the most enlightening information on the situation of the person concerned, and which would be the most serviceable. Here is what I discovered:

• The moment when a person phones is often related to his or her birth chart (see chapter 9). In particular, aspects thrown to the radical chart by the Ascendant, MC, Sun and Moon of the horary chart for the phone call, seem to provide an insight into the motive of that call. More than once, the radical house in which the horary Moon was found revealed the topic of the conversation.

• The moment fixed for the consultation quite often gave marvelous information on the course of the developments in which the client was involved—especially when the client arrived on time.

• The moment when we actively started the interpretation often had a point of contact with the radical chart, but that was about all.

• If there was a big difference between the time of the appointment and the moment the client arrived, the chart for the latter seemed to give far and away the best results; even to the extent that I could rely on it entirely and forget the other charts. So when, in what follows, I refer to the consultation horoscope, I shall mean the chart of the moment when the client walks into the consulting room.

A problem can arise when two people call for a consultation at the same time; however, this seldom occurs.

The rules for a consultation horoscope are exactly the same as those for an ordinary horary chart. Everything discussed earlier still applies. However, a few things seem to be important enough in practice to deserve extra attention—namely:

• *Planets in the 1st house*. These indicate circumstances that will quickly arise or develop. These planets should also be studied in their capacities as house rulers, *with* the aspects they make.

• *The house in which the Moon stands*. All sorts of development, and generally changes, too, take place in the areas of life represented by this house. For example: with the Moon in 4, we may expect a move, rebuilding, or a change in the composition of the family, etc.

• *The house in which the ruler of 1 is posited*. This house requires special attention. In many cases the querent seems to be much occupied with the things it represents.

• *The house in which Mercury stands*. The area covered by this house can also be one that figures prominently in the querent's world of ideas. In the same way, the house in which Saturn stands may represent the sources of the client's problems and anxieties.

• *The Ascendant of the consultation horoscope*. This falls in a certain house of the radix and, in general, that house seems to be important. Also aspects from the MC and Ascendant of the consultation horoscope to planets and points in the radix seem to be valuable for the interpretation. Even intermediate cusps of the horary chart conjunct radical planets or points provide some information.

I have very often observed that personal progressions and transits are apt to point in the same direction as do those of the consultation horoscope. Primary and secondary progressions are the ones I use, plus, of course, the transits. Thus, in a client's progressions for a certain year, I saw the possibility of a love affair or marriage suggested by harmonious primary directions of the ruler of 7 and Venus. But, in the horary chart of the moment for which her consultation had been booked, there was no sign of anything to do with love or marriage. In preparing for the interview, I felt puzzled, because it was something new in my experience. The reason for the discrepancy did not become clear until the day of the appointment: the consultation did not take place because the client suddenly fell sick and the horary chart went by the board. The later consultation horoscope did in fact point to a relationship, which accordingly materialized.

The Horary Consultation Chart and Personal Progressions

I shall now illustrate how certain horary charts and the personal horoscope can hang together and what role the consultation horoscope can play in this. Let's work with the following lengthy example.

The woman concerned (Chart 11 on page 142) is herself at home in astrology, but she wanted to exchange ideas with me over her

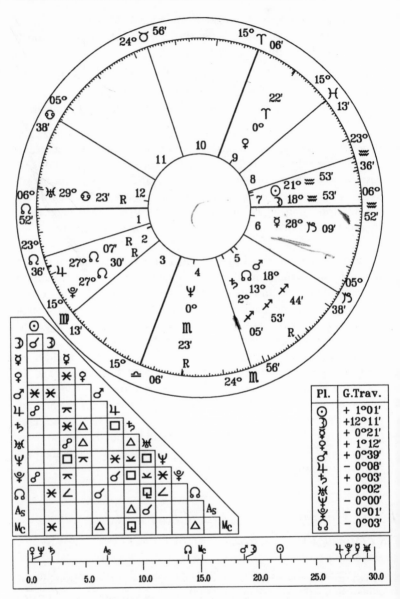

Chart 11. Natal chart for the translator. Lekkerkerk, Holland (51 N 54, 4 E 41), February 11, 1956, 3:14:12 P.M. GMT. Placidus houses. Chart calculated by Astrolabe using *Nova Printwheels*.

horoscope and progressions. She told me that she was unable to find her métier, was always searching for something to satisfy her, and felt she was living in a kind of vacuum. She was studying English and needed to take just two more (big) examinations for her degree. She was in possession of her papers as an interpreter/translator. But she did not really want to be an interpreter—translating was too tedious and quiet for her—and she was even less motivated to pursue her studies. She had been neglecting them for some time, and meanwhile had been working for an agency supplying temporary secretaries, but did not wish to keep doing this. In addition, she had relationship problems and her emotions were in a turmoil. "What shall I do now?" she asked me. "I am tired of the whole sorry mess; I spoil all my relationships, and I have the feeling that I have gotten myself into a hole from which there is no getting out."

Not long before she phoned me, she had gone to a psychiatrist who used the Gestalt method, for she definitely wanted to do something about her situation. Look at the horary chart of the moment when she rang me (Chart 12 on p. 144). Cancer is on the Ascendant, and the degree is one that tends to make judgment unsafe. But the degree on the Ascendant makes an exact square with her radical Venus and a trine with radical Neptune. This means that the chart is in fact open to interpretation.

In all respects, Venus has to do with the expression of our affections and with love affairs. The client had already told me about her problems over the latter during our phone conversation, and what she said was borne out by the horary Ascendant's square to radical Venus.

The horary Ascendant also makes a trine to radical Neptune. Neptune is the ruler of her 9th house, the house that is concerned with study. This was also discussed on the phone. It is worth noting that the aspect is very exact—less than a one degree orb.

The Moon in the horary chart for the moment she phoned (Chart 12) is just inside the 12th house of her birth chart (Chart 11), and the Ascendant of this horary chart is just inside her 11th house. Where relationships were concerned, she alluded not only to love affairs, but also to friendships; which certainly fits in with a horary Ascendant in her radical 11th house. But the effect of the Moon in her 12th house was even more dire. The horary Moon in the radical horoscope often forms a very important indication, and here it called attention to the role of her 12th house. This house appears to be very significant in her

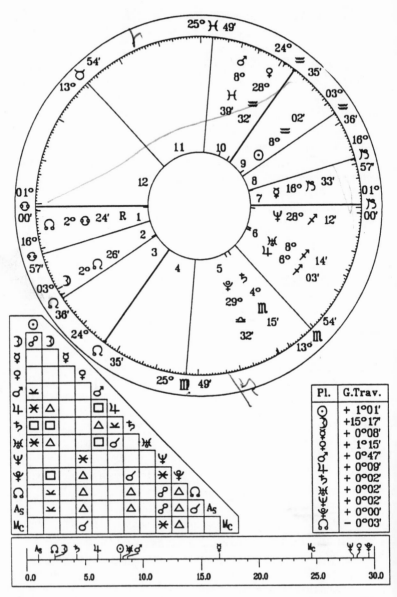

Chart 12. Horary chart for the translator. Amsterdam, Holland (52 N 22, 4 E 54), January 28, 1983, 12:59 P.M. GMT. Placidus houses. Chart calculated by Astrolabe using *Nova Printwheels*.

birth chart in any case. So let us digress for a while, in order to take a closer look at the lady's birth chart (Chart 11).

In this birth chart, we see that Uranus is in the 12th house, and that the Moon is ruler of that house (Cancer is on cusp 12). I have repeatedly been driven to the conclusion that what a child undergoes in the last stage of pregnancy and in infancy, can be found in the 12th house and in the place of the ruler of the 12th house. Uranus in 12 points to past tensions, either between the parents themselves, or between the parents and others; alternatively, one of the parents may have been suffering from strain. Whatever the details of the situation, anything of this sort is bound to be disturbing, and even a source of anxiety, to the child. The ruler of the 12th house is in this lady's 7th house, and conjunct her radical Sun.

The ruler of 12 conjunct the Sun is something I have encountered, times without number, in the birth charts of children whose fathers played hardly any part in their lives when they were very young; perhaps because the fathers were always away from home — on business trips, or as seamen, for example — and had little chance to see their children grow up. Another possibility is that the fathers were dead, or were hospitalized for a long time following an accident, or the like. Alternatively, if the father did live at home, he may have spent most of the time in his study, or he may have been psychologically unapproachable, or always drunk. Then again, the mother may have inwardly had many problems with the father. Whatever the case may be, the Lord of 12 conjunct the Sun means, all too often, that in infancy the child was unable to form a father-image. And infancy is more important than we think. This is the period when the majority of connections between the brain cells are made that form the matrix for our later functioning. If something goes wrong at this time, it can have grave consequences for our subsequent emotional life and behavior. Something of the sort appears to have happened with this lady: her father was an alcoholic who did not begin to get the better of his habit until she was 3 years old — a situation that seems to be clearly associated with her ruler of 12 conjunct the Sun.

The Sun in her chart is important for the picture she forms, and for the pattern of expectations developed of her future life partner. Quite frequently I have seen women with the Lord of 12 conjunct the Sun having difficulties here. Either they did not know how to behave in a relationship, or they did not know precisely what attracted them to the other person; and perhaps there were other problems connected with an incompletely formed, sometimes chaotic, picture of what they wanted their partner to be and do.

The lady's current problems with partnership clearly had to do with the unhappy situation in her early youth. But not all the blame is to be laid at the door of the Sun conjunct the ruler of 12. There is also the presence of the Lord of 12 in her 7th house; which means that she is looking for a heavenly and idealistic marriage, in which she can sink her own interests on behalf of the other person. But what I see, all too often, in this position, is expectations that are too rosy, and a partner who is idealized excessively, or put on a pedestal wearing a halo; all of which stands in the way of a genuine personal relationship, because the other is not seen and accepted as a human being, but is treated as if clothed in some sort of divinity. Sooner or later, this is bound to lead to disappointment, when the other person stands revealed as only human. And when the partner falls off the pedestal, the person with the Lord of 12 in 7 thinks that this partner is unsuitable, *or* is much altered. Of course, this is generally not true; it is the projection which has undergone alteration. Whatever else we may say, it must be admitted that very idealistic and spiritual relationships can flourish with the Lord of 12 in 7, but in many instances a chaotic element will be introduced as a result of the idealizing being too strong initially. Turning again to our example, we see a situation there in which the formation of an ideal image of the partner and of the marriage plays a part. Therefore we should pay special attention to the 12th house in the consultation horoscope, other horary charts and in her progressions in order to see what is happening there. There lies the key. The fact that the Moon of the horary chart cast for the moment of the phone call (Chart 12) is in the radical 12th house, is a very clear indication that we need to look closely at this house.

In the horary chart of the moment of phoning, Mercury is in Capricorn and, when transferred to the birth chart, it falls in the 6th house. Mercury often reveals an important part of the conversation in phone calls, and in this case the client's work was one of the topics. Thus we find one or two useful indications in the relationship between the phone-call chart and the birth chart, namely:

• The horary Ascendant within a one-degree orb of an exact trine to the radical ruler of 9, and square radical Venus,

• The horary Moon in the radical 12th house,

- The horary Ascendant in the radical 11th house,

- The horary Mercury in the radical 6th house.

And there is one more intriguing point of contact. Her progressed Ascendant was in 24° Leo, a degree that we shall find on the cusp of the 4th house, or IC, of the chart of the phone call (Chart 12). She came for the appointment exactly on time; see Chart 13 on page 148 — our consultation horoscope. In the outer circle of this horoscope are the positions of the cusps for the moment we started the interpretation. To begin with we sat and talked, as we had known one another for years.

The precise moment when we began gave several points of contact with her birth chart:

- The horary Ascendant trine her radical Sun within a 1° orb;

- Horary cusp 6 conjunct radical Neptune;

- Horary MC exactly sextile radical MC;

- Her secondary Moon was precisely at the place in her radix where the MC stood at the moment of commencement;

- The North Node has reached the place where the Ascendant of the horary chart for the time of phoning stood, and therefore makes the same aspects as the Ascendant did then — trine radical Neptune and square radical Venus. This focuses attention on these planets, which had a very direct bearing on the questions the client had.

I was not surprised that the North Node was prominent. Important relationships, as well as our inner sense of destiny, always belong to the terrain of the North Node, and these did indeed form this woman's main problem at this moment.

Now let us take a look at some of the problems that had to be considered. She had already mentioned over the phone that she had been taking part in group therapy; but, during the consultation, she made no secret of the fact that she was very unhappy with the treatment. She felt that she had no contact with the therapist, who seemed to be very aloof. She also thought that he did not understand her problem, but relied largely on his routines and techniques and on little else. She felt that this was a great pity. What is more, the therapist did not wish to explain the reasons for some of the things he

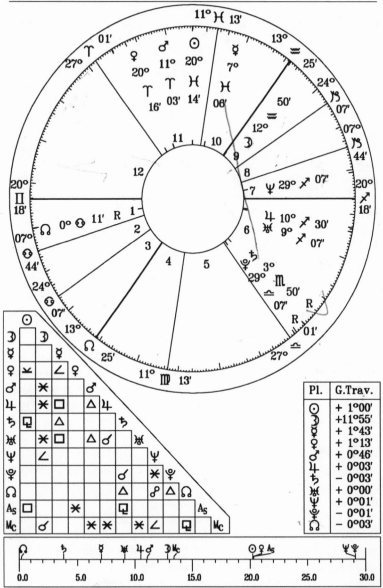

Chart 13. The time the client arrived for the consultation. Amsterdam, Holland (52 N 22, 4 E 54), March 11, 1983, 9:30 A.M. GMT. Placidus houses. Chart calculated by Astrolabe using *Nova Printwheels*.

did. Her Sun in Aquarius shows that she is the sort of person who expects to be treated as an equal and to be given sensible explanations before being prepared to proceed. She added that, if only she knew how it was supposed to work, she would be quite prepared to take the plunge and let herself go emotionally; but, because he did not tell her anything, she clammed up and became more frustrated than ever. Anyway, she had the feeling that the whole thing had become a blind alley.

In the horary chart for the moment she arrived (Chart 13), her significator is Mercury and her cosignificator is the Moon. We see, in this chart, that Mercury has made a trine to Saturn, which here is the significator of the therapist, because Capricorn in on cusp 8. The trine has already been exact, and this shows that contact has already taken place. But Saturn is retrograde, indicating that the therapist can do little for this client. As we discussed in the paragraph on retrograde planets, the person indicated by a retrograde planet has nothing much to contribute to the matter, withdraws from it, or relinquishes his or her claims, withholds information or fails to see things as they are. However good this therapist might be, he was unable to help the client much. There is a negative indication in this chart as far as therapy is concerned. This indication was substantiated by the horoscope of the moment when we actually started the consultation.

The client herself practiced astrology, and she thought of making a horary chart for the moment when she and the therapist first met for an introductory talk (Chart 14 on page 150). Here we have an event chart and not the horary chart of a question. So the first thing we have to do is discover which party took the initiative, since the 1st house belongs to that person. She was the one who had made the inquiries about therapy, so she is in the 1st house.

Because the Ascendant is in the first degrees of its sign, the opportunities for making a judgment are limited. "It is still too early to tell," is what the Ascendant in such an early degree is saying. However, within a one-degree orb, the Ascendant is making a contact with her radix—an opposition to Saturn, in fact—which can point to difficulties. Let us judge the chart carefully.

The psychiatrist falls in the 8th house. Sagittarius is on cusp 8, so Jupiter is the psychiatrist's significator. Neptune is posited in 8 and is his co-significator. Mercury at 2° 21′ Aquarius is sextile Jupiter at 2° 03′ Sagittarius, a sextile which has just been exact. This represents their previous contact by phone, leading to the introductory talk. This

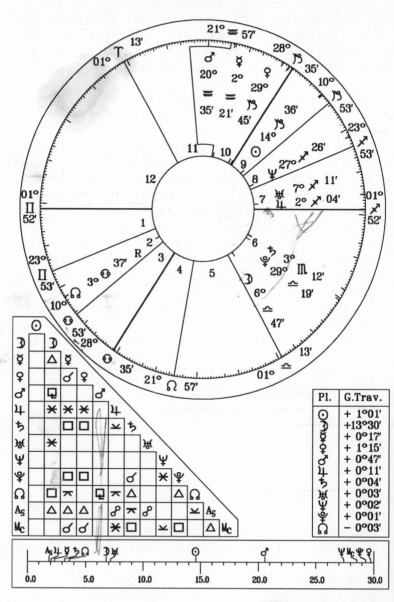

Chart 14. The event chart when client met therapist. Amsterdam, Holland (52 N 22, 4 E 54), January 5, 1983, 12:45 P.M. GMT. Placidus houses. Chart calculated by Astrolabe using *Nova Printwheels.*

positive aspect, which shows there was a favorable impression, lies in the past. Also, the sextile between the Moon and Jupiter lies in the past. On the other hand, there are problem areas in the chart. If we use the average orb of 6° for major aspects (and 4° for sextiles), Mars makes no major aspect in the chart. This points to wasted energy, or poor management of the therapy, or something of the sort. An unaspected planet behaves very erratically: one moment it is strong and another moment it is weak. Every now and then, its influence suddenly makes itself felt in an exaggerated way. Therefore the danger of quarrels or differences of opinion is present in this chart; also the danger that one or the other of the parties will misapply their efforts. Besides, Mars is Lord of the 12th house in the chart, an important house for this woman. The fact that the Lord of 12 is unaspected can mean that the therapy does not uncover part of the psyche. Possibly this is not the correct form of therapy or therapist for her.

A second point is that her significator, Mercury, is about to turn retrograde. Apart from anything else, this is an indication that she is going to sit back and take stock of the situation, that she will reconsider it and see it in a different light, and in general, "pull out." But, by turning retrograde, Mercury moves once more in the direction of the therapist's significator, Jupiter. Clearly there is still a chance of positive contact, although not in such a way that the client would have any grip on the situation—this is not possible when a significator is retrograde. She made it perfectly plain to me how dissatisfied she was with the state of affairs. A week later she spoke her mind about the situation during the therapy session, and stated that she could not go on in the same way and wanted to stop. And then something happened that took her by surprise: her therapist treated her in the way she had wanted him to treat her, and suddenly explained everything to her. This threw her into confusion; and yet it is precisely what might have been expected from the sextile between the two indicators becoming exact once more. Even so, she was not mollified, and cancelled the treatment then and there: the retrograde party withdrew.

Looking at the aspects made by the Moon before quitting her sign, we see the following: a sextile to Uranus, a square to the Sun, a trine to Mars, a contraparallel to Pluto, a sextile to Neptune, and a conjunction with Pluto. The last major aspect made by the Moon is always important. With the Moon conjunct Pluto we have, in one way or another, a strained situation again. The confrontation is by no means over, and this points to problems in therapy.

Stmk

At the moment when these conflicts came to a head, Pluto was transiting 29° Libra in her birth chart and became stationary, greatly increasing its influence in the process. This transit made an exact square to her radical Uranus, the Lord of 8 in her horoscope. Pluto, the planet of conflicts, of power struggles and of bringing everything hidden to light, was clearly highlighting the field of tension between her and her therapist.

We have now seen that her birth chart, the horary chart of the moment of phoning, the chart of the moment she stepped into my office, the chart of the moment when we started the consultation, and the chart of her introductory conference with her psychiatrist, *all displayed the same theme, namely difficulties with the therapist*! All these apparently isolated moments actually hang together. It seems as if things happen only at their own, appropriate moments.

Another important consideration was her studies. Various indications were present in her primary directions and secondary progressions that appeared to favor the continuation of her studies, although Saturn was impeding them by transiting backward and forward over radical Neptune, Lord of 9, the house of higher education. In the consultation horoscope (Chart 13 of page 148), we find that the 9th house falls in Capricorn, and that Saturn here represents not only her therapist, but also her studies. This retrograde Saturn signified an unfortunate situation with her therapist, while Saturn here was of great benefit to her studies. A retrograde planet signifies the return to an old situation and, in this case, it would mean the picking up of the thread of her studies. Mercury, her significator, coming parallel with Saturn is a positive indication for the return to her old studies—outstandingly so in fact!

Also in the horary chart cast for the moment of phoning, we see that after a square to Saturn, the Moon makes the following aspects one after another: a contra- or split parallel to Uranus, a trine to Jupiter, a trine to Uranus, an opposition to the Sun, a contraparallel to Jupiter, a contraparallel to Mercury, a contraparallel to the Sun, a trine to Neptune, and a sextile to Pluto. In this chart, Uranus is Lord of 9 and therefore the significator of her studies. We see in prospect a positive link between the Moon, as her significator, and Uranus, as the significator of her studies; first through the contraparallel (although there is perhaps some slight doubt about this), and then shortly after through a trine. The succession of the aspects seems to show that first of all she has to put the difficulties with the therapist behind her (the square to Saturn) before making a new, but hesitating, start; that she will then make an important decision with regard to her work, because the Moon is going to make a trine to Jupiter and Jupiter is co-ruler of 6, and that *then* her studies can be resumed. The last aspect is a sextile to Pluto, which holds the promise of a good outcome.

Another problem area was her relationship. She was fond of a young man, but she was not his only girlfriend, although she was high on his list of favorites. He did not want to make a permanent commitment or take any responsibility for or in the relationship. She wondered whether she could go on in this way. For this and other reasons, the relationship was under a lot of strain. At the end of 1982, and several times in 1983, Saturn transits backward and forward in Scorpio. Also it transits Neptune, Lord of her 9th, which indicates problems with her studies. But, at the same time, Saturn, by transit, is inconjunct her Venus, and this puts a tiresome brake on the expression of affection. With such a transit, one often sees that the person concerned feels an inner block and finds it difficult to be loving; but also that the period is one of circumstances that make it hard to express feelings of love and friendship freely and easily. The inconjunct engenders the feeling that there is no control over the situation, but that the individual has his or her back against the wall.

There is something more that can be said about this transit picture. Pluto and Saturn are moving backward and forward over the last degrees of Libra, and coming into conflict with Mercury and Uranus. The latter are in opposition in the radix (see Chart 12 on page 144), so Pluto and Saturn make a temporary t-square with them during this transit. This produces a strong field of tension that demands resolution. Matters are made even more acute for this woman because Uranus is the ruler of her 7th house, the house of partnerships, and also of her 8th, which has to do with unconscious factors affecting the way she functions in a relationship. The animus of a woman and the anima of a man will always be found in the 8th house.

Pluto is ruler of the 5th, the house of romance and the like; thus the transit is most applicable to the situation. She has a man-friend with whom she wants a settled relationship, but he is unwilling to go along with this. In transit, the Lord of 5 is square the Lord of 7 and 8 to give the powerful effect of Saturn in the temporary t-square that makes the situation even more critical. Neptune, too, has a finger in the pie, by hovering around a conjunction with Uranus, the ruler of her 7th and 8th. This brings a danger of disillusionment, of the misty and chaotic element in the relationship and the difficult course of affairs.

However, at almost the same time, transiting Neptune makes a trine to Jupiter and Pluto. This favors her studies, for Neptune is her Lord of 9. These transit aspects can soften the hard action of Saturn on her radical Neptune.

By primary progression, Pluto, Lord of 5, is inconjunct the native's radical Moon and square Mars—not a hopeful indication for a flexible and smooth functioning of the lovelife. By secondary progression, we find the same aspect as in the transit, namely an inconjunct of secondary Venus to radical Saturn. All these indications make it highly probable that the difficulties in the relationship will continue for the time being. This needs to be confirmed by the horary chart.

In Chart 12 (page 144) for the moment she phoned, we see the following possibilities. The relationship is one that is important to her and she wants to remain close to the one she loves. For this, we must examine the 7th house. But the relationship has not progressed as far as this; so we also need to look at the 5th. In this chart, the Lord of 5 is Mercury. There is no positive applying aspect between the Moon, the lady's significator, and Mercury, her friend's significator; what is more, Mercury stands on cusp 8. A planet on a cusp means that the person signified by it is about to experience a change. The 8th house is the 4th of the 5th, and so Mercury—representing the friend—is on the point of entering its 4th house. Frequently, the 4th house has to do with the end of things and, in this case, can mean a breaking or ending of the relationship.

Now, if we take the lady's Lord of 7 in horary Chart 12 (page 144) we note that the significator is Saturn, the same significator as for the psychiatrist. The Moon is making an applying square to Saturn, and this is a further warning of the danger of a break. In fact, a break had already taken place, *before* she came to me.

Turning to consultation Chart 13 on page 148, set for the moment the client walked in, we also see the break depicted. Jupiter, the Lord of the 7th house, and therefore one of the possible significators of her friend, is just leaving a conjunction with Uranus. A combination of this sort invariably points to hidden tensions. But Mercury, the lady's significator, is heading toward further tension with an applying square to this Uranus and this Jupiter. The native was wondering whether or not it would be a good idea to try and get back together with her friend, in spite of the break. The applying aspect certainly shows that a new contact is possible, but also that it will be rather disappointing and liable to end in another break. This is all the more likely because Mercury is Lord of 5 as well, and therefore is the significator of her friend. Obviously, the progressions in the different charts present the same picture.

Of course, much more was discussed during our talk—too much to be repeated here—but I hope that enough has been said to show how we can use the Consultation Chart and the Horary Chart of a phone call as additional means of understanding a situation and for putting progressions in perspective. At the same time, they will give us an insight (even if only a modest one) into the connection of things as reflected in the interrelationship of the radix, on the one hand, and the progressions and horary charts for seemingly arbitrary moments on the other. Each moment in our lives is linked with moments before and after, but each moment on its own has something specific to say to us.

Will I meet The Right man For
A good Relationship ?
11:11Am 10/18/95

What Shall I do enbances my
WRiting & Speaking abilities ?
11:44 am 10/18/95

11

Practical Examples

Horary charts can be cast for all kinds of questions and events. The point on which everything turns is how to make a correct choice of significator for the quesited or for the event being studied. There are fixed rules of interpretation in horary astrology for things such as the sale and purchase of movables or real estate, for lost articles, legacies, trips, and so on. In this chapter we shall look at several of these. But first, I want to remind readers that a question and its answer are not usually confined to a single house. Even if the quesited, itself, falls in a single house, other houses often enter in as representatives of the place of the significator and its aspects, the place of the querent, etc. Therefore it is not always easy to give a rule-of-thumb by which houses may be assigned to particular questions. As we shall see, a house that is characteristic of a certain type of question is often just a starting point and not our sole guide. So, in this chapter, the discussion will center on a number of themes together with the rules governing them, and on any connections within the horary chart.

I shall also endeavor to demonstrate that we can always cast horary charts, whatever the position of the planets in the sky. In the early 80s, I was quite often asked whether or not all answers would be much the same in periods when most planets were bunched together in a small section of the zodiac, or in periods when the slow-moving planets were near a cusp. Hence in this chapter and also elsewhere in the book, I have tried to select the examples from a time-span that is as short as possible, in order to show that nothing happening in the heavens detracts from the usefulness of horary astrology provided we keep to the rules.

Buying and Selling

In questions concerning buying and selling, the angles always play an important role. The 1st house invariably represents the querent, no matter who is buyer or seller. The 7th house is that of the other party. The 4th house represents the item for which a change of ownership is being proposed, and the 10th house has to do with the price.

Some horary astrologers (e.g., Raphael) think that the seller always lies in the 1st house and the buyer in the 7th—others take the opposite view. In my experience this is a mistake: I have found that the querent always falls in the 1st house, whether he or she is buyer or seller.

A number of small points need to be observed in any question concerning buying and selling; but, naturally, attention must first of all be paid to the basic rules of horary interpretation. First of all, we look to see whether or not a sale will take place; in other words, we look for a connection between houses 1 and 7 or between Moon and the 7th house. If none, we may as well lay the chart aside. If one, we can examine it further.

Money is important in buying and selling. We must look at the significators of both parties. If the Lord of 1 is the stronger, or if the Lord of 1 is in 1, the gain will go to the querent. If the Lord of 7 is the stronger, or if the Lord of 7 is in 7, then the other party has the advantage.

If the other party is the seller and if his or her significator is not well placed or aspected, the signs are that he or she is in difficulties and badly in need of cash. This is usually an indication of a somewhat lower price. But further information about the price will be found in the 10th house. Care is needed with the interpretation: Jupiter in 10 does not necessarily mean that the price will be good, and Saturn in 10 does not necessarily mean that the price will be low. Everything depends on the situation. Generally speaking, Jupiter in 10 suggests that the price is much too high, or that the item is a status symbol for which people are prepared to pay more than the value. Jupiter in the 2nd house can speak the same message and, according to some, the same applies when house 2 has Sagittarius or Pisces (the signs traditionally ruled by Jupiter) on the cusp.

Saturn in the 10th house can mean a low price, and that can be very advantageous to the purchaser! And we must watch out for Mars in 10; the price really slumps then. It is as if Mars cuts a piece out of the price. So if we want to sell our house, and Mars stands in the 10th house of the horary chart, we had better wait. Unfortunately, we may find ourselves in circumstances where there is no time to wait and we need the money urgently; in such cases, we must be prepared to drop the price.

Also, the Lord of 10 may be weakly placed and not in an angle, in which case the price is often low once more. If, in addition, the Lord of 10 has hard aspects, this is another indication that the seller is anxious to obtain some money. In itself, this has nothing to do with the quality of what is offered; for that we have to look at the significators of the personal property or real estate, as the case may be.

Generally, if the Lord of 10 is fortified and/or angular, the price holds up and may even be on the high side. But if, within a few days (at most within a week) of the question being asked, the ruler of the 10th house turns retrograde, the price will change. And the price almost always changes when Mercury turns retrograde, wherever it stands and whether or not it is the significator. Because Mercury represents the mind, the parties change their minds about the price and about the course of the negotiations.

Something else that needs to be remembered concerning price, is the risk of deception or fraud. This risk seems to be great when Neptune is in 10 or when a malefic is in the 7th house (unless it is Lord of 7). Then the other party plays a (very crafty) game. The same may also be true when the Lord of 10 or the Lord of 7 is weakly placed and retrograde. Confirmatory evidence in the chart is required, but at least we should be on our guard. Also, hard aspects of the Moon with the MC, with the Lord of 4 or with planets in 4, increase the likelihood of extra, unforeseen costs. In any case, hard aspects of the Moon always presage disappointments. And here we must not overlook the Moon's last aspect before quitting the sign she occupies; for at least some disappointment will occur if this aspect is hard. The same applies (although, in my experience, to a lesser extent) if the Moon's last

8th H. margin 2nd H

aspect is made to a retrograde planet. In this instance, the type of aspect is not so important: what is indicated is that progress will be slowed down or possibly brought to a standstill.

If the item being placed on sale is expensive, financing can be important, therefore look at the following possibilities. If, as the seller, we want to know if the buyer can meet his or her obligations, we must first of all examine the buyer's 2nd house; this is the 8th house in the chart, because the 7th is the buyer's 1st house. It has to be judged as we judge everything in a horary chart. A good 8th house means that the finances are sound.

When we are the purchaser, our own financial situation is shown by the 2nd house. But when our outlay is large and we have to take out a loan or a mortgage, then it is the 8th house that needs to be analyzed.

There is something else to bear in mind when we evaluate the financial situation, and that is the need to make a correct identification of the house in which the purchase item falls. Suppose we want to buy a residence: in that event, we have to study the 4th astrological house—unless we already own or rent a home, in which case our intended purchase is our next home and will fall in the 4th house from the 4th, namely in house 7 of the chart. Taking the analysis still further, we can look at the 2nd house of the 4th from the 4th, i.e., at the 2nd from the 7th, the 8th in the chart. This can shed light on the financial progress of the transaction. If it is in good shape, then the financial affairs will prove satisfactory. But if Saturn is posited in it, beware!

Let's look at another example. If we want to buy a ring or some other personal item, the rule is to look at the 2nd house; but, if we are buying a replacement, the situation is the same as in moving to a new home. In the example just mentioned, the 2nd house would represent the old ring and the 2nd house from the 2nd would represent the new ring. And the 2nd one again gives the financial consequences of the acquisition. Thus for the simple purchase of a ring we look at 2, and for a replacement ring we look at 3. And for the financial circumstances surrounding the purchase of the replacement ring, we look at the 2nd house from the 3rd, which is the 4th house of the chart. This all sounds rather complicated, I know, but it is well worth mastering.

If we want to buy something for ourselves, it is a good sign when the 2nd house of the chart is favorable, for that means no losses. However, if the North Node is in 2, the purchase can produce problems.

To know if an object is in good condition, look at the situation of the house in which the object falls. A piece of personal property falls in the 2nd house. While we are thinking of buying an object, it still belongs to someone else and, to judge its condition, we have to look at the 2nd house from the 7th—i.e., at the 8th. But, for a residence belonging to someone else, we must look at the 4th house from the 7th—i.e., at the 10th. Planets in that house and the ruler of that house can help us in making a final decision. Thus, if these are essentially dignified, there will be no harm in making the purchase.

A final point that could be important in charts erected for buying and selling is the role of any intermediary. In the sale and purchase of a house, this is usually a real estate agent. This person falls in the 2nd house of the chart. Planets in 2 and the Lord of 2 can inform us about the activities and professional ability of the agent. On several occasions, I have observed that a real estate agent signified by a retrograde Lord of 2 did nothing to promote the sale, or withheld information, or seemed untrustworthy, or something of the sort. Also, a debilitated Lord of 2 often means that the agent is unable to do much. Because, in some cases, the agent can make all the difference to the transaction, it pays to analyze the house in which he or she falls.[1]

Let us look at horary Chart 15 (page 162). A woman asked me if she would be able to sell her house. In the horary chart, her significators are Mercury and the Moon. A potential purchaser is signified by Jupiter and Neptune. The Moon is approaching a square to Neptune. Of course, this does represent a contact of sorts, but not a contact likely to lead to a sale.

---

[1]There is some question as to why the real estate agent would be governed by the 2nd house. In my country, important advisors for money and real estate (possessions and valuables) are placed in the 2nd house. The 5th house represents advisors who have to do with speculation and the stockmarket, while the 9th house indicates advisors on issues that have to do with legislation, legal affairs, the law, and legalization. The 7th house contains "the other party," and "the other advisor who is your equal," when you are unable to put this person elsewhere in the horary chart. I have found that this particular breakdown works when we do horary charts, but students will have to explore this concept for themselves.

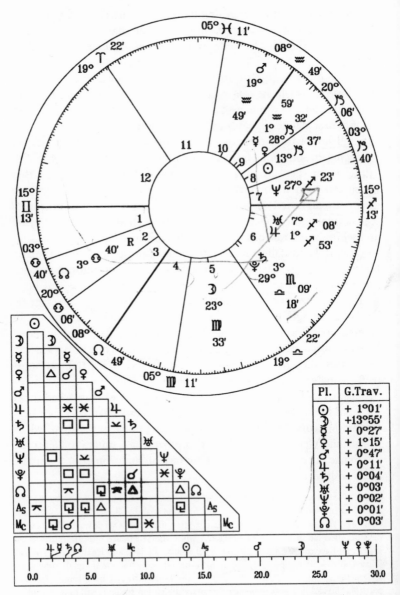

Chart 15. Will I sell my house? Amsterdam, Holland (52 N 22, 4 E 54), January 4, 1983, 1:31 P.M. GMT. Placidus houses. Chart calculated by Astrolabe using *Nova Printwheels*.

Mercury, her other significator, is leaving a sextile to Jupiter; but this suggests that the opportunity for making a sale has already occurred or, at least, that someone has been interested. However, the aspect is no longer partile, and therefore represents something that is no longer in prospect. On the basis of these two indications, we can draw the tentative conclusion that there is no promise of a sale in the chart.

Now note the following. On referring to the ephemeris, we see that Mercury turns retrograde on January 7th (the question was asked on January 4, 1983) and renews its sextile to Jupiter, the significator of the purchaser. This, in itself, ought to indicate a sale. Nevertheless, we should not be too hopeful, because a retrograde significator fails to live up to expectations (often through force of circumstances) and, in the present case, this can mean that the seller will have to be satisfied with a lower offer. Her financial picture is far from rosy and she needs money so urgently that she may be forced to reduce her price for a quick sale. Mars in the 10th house points in the same direction, and the traditional Lord of her 10th house, Saturn, is at 3° 08′ Scorpio, the same degree as the North Node (in Cancer)! What is more, Saturn is in a cadent house, not a favorable position for the Lord of 10, since the Lord of 10 has a bearing on the amount paid.

All in all, the horary chart suggests that the lady will in fact find a buyer, but that she will have to make do with a (very) low price. The question is whether or not she will find this acceptable.

The real estate agent is symbolized here by the Moon, as ruler of 2, and the Moon is approaching a square to Neptune. There is a risk of deception on the part of the real estate agent—something she had already found out at the time of the question. Neptune in 7 also indicates this. The buyer has sufficient funds, because the Sun is in the 8th house, the 2nd from the 7th, the buyer's money house.

The woman was in a very awkward predicament and the sale of her house was a bitter pill for her to swallow. Look at the critical degrees. Both the MC/IC axis and the Lord of 4, the Sun, are in a critical degree (see chapter 6, section 3)!

The woman did receive an offer for her house, but the offer was absurdly low. And, although she was in need, she refused it, because she felt she would only be worse off in the end. During the active life of the horary chart (which, on average, would be about three months) she had no success in selling her house.

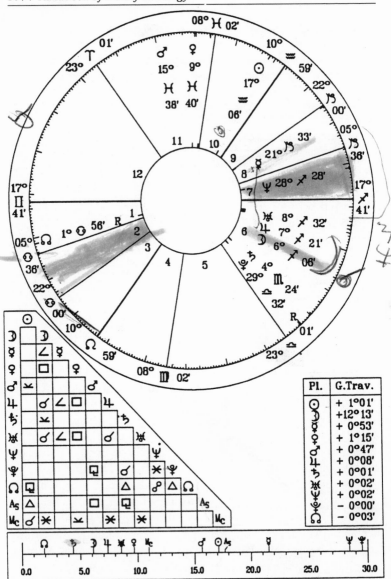

Chart 16. Will I make money at this trade fair? Amsterdam, Holland (52 N 22, 4 E 54), February 6, 1983, 11:30 A.M. GMT. Placidus houses. Chart calculated by Astrolabe using *Nova Printwheels*.

Employment and Business Affairs

Questions are often asked about work and business matters. People want to know if they will get the job, or whether they will be able to make the most of a business opportunity. A few examples will show how to deal with such questions.

Horary Chart 16 is the chart of an antiquarian bookseller who was wondering how he would do at an internationally important book fair for the second-hand trade. The querent is signified by Mercury and the Moon. Potential buyers and sellers at the fair fall under 7, and their significators are Jupiter and Neptune. The Moon is in 6, and this was appropriate in view of the fact that the question had to do with the gentleman's work. It is significant that the Moon is making an applying conjunction with Jupiter, the significator of the other party. It is therefore very certain that business will be transacted.

The business had to do with books, and books fall under Mercury and the 3rd house. In the present case, the ruler of the 3rd house is the Moon. So the Moon and Mercury are not only the significators of the querent, but also the significators of his trade. It is always an advantage for the querent when the significators are the same: he has a grip on the whole situation.

Our possessions lie in the 2nd house, but the sale-value of our possessions lies in the 3rd! Therefore planets in 3 and the Lord of 3 can give us further information about this. In the present instance, the Moon as ruler of 3 is approaching a conjunction with Jupiter, which means that if the querent purchases stock, its value will be high or will become high. Such an aspect usually indicates an increase in the value of our acquisitions.

Finally, we must take a look at the further aspects made by the Moon. In fairly quick succession, the Moon is conjunct Jupiter, conjunct Uranus, square Venus, parallel Jupiter, parallel Mercury, square Mars, sextile the sun, parallel Uranus, parallel Neptune, conjunct Neptune and sextile Pluto. In addition, a parallel is formed between Mercury and Jupiter—another link between the querent and a third party or third parties. The final aspect of the Moon (to Pluto) is harmonious and therefore favorable. Now Pluto is retrograde, which would normally be interpreted as less favorable, but the chart as a whole is so positive that the querent may expect to do good business.

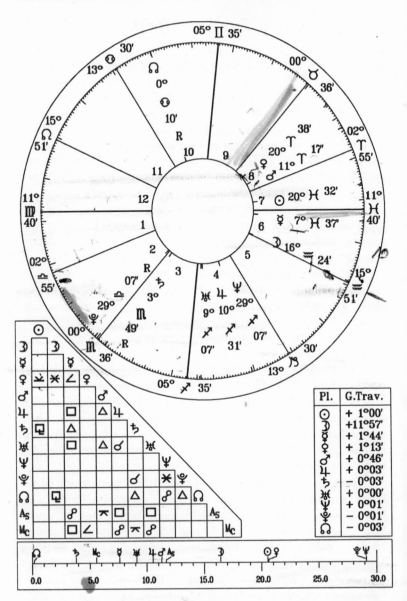

Chart 17. Will my sister-in-law get the job? Amsterdam, Holland (52 N 22, 4 E 54), March 11, 1983, 4:40:30 P.M. GMT. Placidus houses. Chart calculated by Astrolabe using *Nova Printwheels*.

The significator of the other party, Jupiter, occupies the 12th house from the 7th, which is less favorable for this party. Thus we may expect that the advantage will be with the querent rather than with the other party; and, in fact, the querent did do good business.

Chart 17 has to do with obtaining work. The woman who asked the question had heard that her sister-in-law had applied for employment for the umpteenth time, and was anxious to know whether she would be successful. The querent falls in the 1st house. Her sister-in-law is her husband's sister, so we must examine the 3rd house from the 7th, which is the 9th in the chart. Since the 9th house is the 1st house of the sister-in-law, the 2nd house in the chart, being the 6th from the 9th, is the sister-in-law's house of work. Taurus is on the 9th cusp (the sister-in-law was a Taurus!) and so Venus is her significator. The 6th from the 9th house falls in Libra, and Venus therefore rules over this, too. The fact that the two significators are the same is a positive indication. The Moon is co-significator of the sister-in-law (because the querent is not the person for whose prospects the chart has been cast), and we note that the Moon is making an applying sextile to Venus, an indication that the job application will be successful. The Moon is in the 10th from the 9th house and thus in an angle as far as the sister-in-law is concerned. This increases the chance that the matters under consideration will be quickly resolved.

The further aspects of the Moon are: a trine to Pluto (planet in the 6th from the 9th house!) and a sextile to Neptune. There is nothing problematical about the Moon's last aspect, so this is another positive indication. The only doubtful factor in this chart is Pluto; this is retrograde in the 6th from the 9th house, which could cause trouble. However, the other indications suggest that the woman will get the position for which she has applied.

Nineteen days later the sister-in-law phoned the querent to say that she had got the job. Pluto retrograde in the sister-in-law's 6th house does seem to have had something of an adverse effect: her former employer had tried to spoil her chances, but had failed.

The Moon is 16° 24′ Aquarius and Venus is 20° 37′ Aries, a difference of 4° 13′. Since the advertiser had announced that someone was needed fairly quickly, I did not think that I should talk in terms of a time-scale of months for the Moon in a fixed sign in a cardinal house. So I chose weeks (the other alternative), and on the basis of the separation between Venus and the Moon suggested that a start in the new job could well be made around four weeks from the date of the

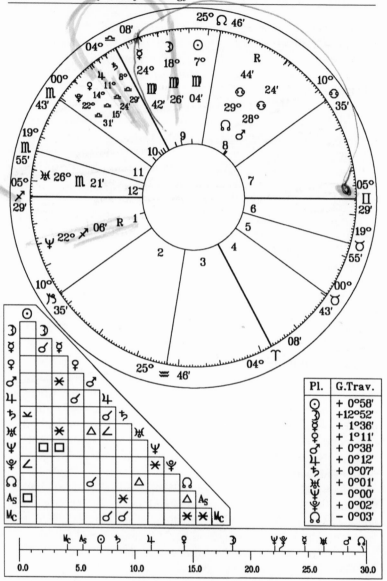

Chart 18. Will my manager leave the business? Amsterdam, Holland (52 N 22, 4 E 54), August 30, 1981, 1:21 P.M. GMT. Placidus houses. Chart calculated by Astrolabe using *Nova Printwheels*.

question. The actual waiting time was three weeks and six days. Although my assessment was fairly accurate, this example illustrates how cautious we must be with time measurements; things do not always work out as we would wish. From an astrological point of view there was one weak point in the chart: Venus, which was the significator both of the sister-in-law and of her work, was in its detriment in Aries. The sister-in-law even appears to have suffered a slight nervous breakdown while she was seeking work. Also there was work she should have done but had never completed even though she had been enthusiastic about it. It is possible that this will continue to cause her a certain amount of trouble. Sometimes a weakly placed ruler signifies that we shall not be doing the particular work for long.

Chart 18 concerned a crisis of confidence between the head of a firm and his manager. The head of the firm asked, "Will my manager leave the business?" The question was ambiguous, because there seemed to have been no formal talk of resignation or dismissal, and the manager had not even hinted that he was wanting to leave. Put on my guard by the presence of retrograde Neptune in the 1st house, I asked the boss if he was withholding information that could be useful in making the interpretation. He replied that, for some considerable time, relations had been strained between him and his manager, although nothing had been said openly. An atmosphere of mistrust had enveloped them, and secretly the head of the firm was hoping that the manager would leave of his own accord, because he felt that this would save the business from being harmed by the tensions. The boss remarked in passing that formerly the manager and he had worked well together, and that he had looked on the man not so much as an employee as a companion and joint policy-maker in the concern.

This particular disclosure is immensely important from the point of view of horary technique: it means that now we do not place the manager in the 6th house of employees but in the 7th house of companions, collaborators, or partners. I have been struck by the fact that the emotional significance attached to someone is decisive for their placement in the houses!

The significators of the querent, the head of the firm, are Jupiter as Lord of 1 and Neptune as the planet in 1, plus, of course, the Moon. The significator of the manager is Mercury. We observe that Mercury has made a square with Neptune; a clear indication of the misunderstandings that had arisen. At the same time, we see Jupiter making a departing aspect with Saturn—a conjunction expressing pressure and difficulties felt by the querent. But the Moon is approaching a conjunction with Mercury, a positive indication for a reconciliation between the two parties.

Neptune in 1 warns that the head of the firm may well be misjudging his manager. With Neptune in 1 there is always a danger that people and situations will be wrongly assessed. With Neptune in 1 things are not always what they seem. The horary chart clearly pointed to renewed contact, which was the very reverse of what the querent expected. There was indeed a renewed contact, and the boss told me later that he had been unaware that, during the period in question, his manager had been going through such a bad time in his private life. If we consider matters from the standpoint of the 7th house in this chart, we shall get an idea of what had been happening to the manager. The 10th house in the chart is his 4th house; and with Saturn and Pluto there, he had been battling with tensions in his family circle. Saturn is the ruler of the 8th from the 7th house (the original 2nd in the chart), and this points to the possibility of bereavement. In fact, a much loved member of the family died, and it took the manager quite a long while to recover from his grief. To make matters worse, Uranus is in the 12th house, which is the 6th from the 7th, or his house of work. Uranus warns of overstrain in this area and, indeed, the manager behaved moodily during the period we are considering; he was very irritable, and at times it was impossible to reason with him. Mars, in the 8th house of the chart is in his own 2nd house, so he had financial problems too, on top of everything else. Owing to this conjunction of circumstances, he had become taciturn and surly. Moreover he was not very approachable at his place of work, so that there was a breakdown in communications. Because he would not say what was wrong, he became estranged from his employer, arousing the mistrust in the latter that eventually led to the chart being cast. However, the two men did finally get back on good terms after the air had been cleared between them.

For partnerships and other forms of business collaboration, we must always look at the 7th house. The querent belongs to the 1st house, and his financial situation to the 2nd. The business partner belongs to 7 and his financial situation to 8. The business, itself, is represented by 10 and its funding by 11.

If we intend going into business with someone, we need to note the following points:

• Whether there is a favorable connection between the 1st and the 7th house or not. This is a prerequisite, because it means that the two partners can pull together. When there is a hard aspect, the result is disunity and tension because the partners have different policies.

• Whether the Lord of 7 or planets in 7 are making hard aspects to the difficult planets Mars, Saturn, Uranus, Neptune, and Pluto, and whether difficult planets are posited in 7. This signifies the danger that cooperation will become something of a problem, or altogether impossible, through the other person's fault.

• Whether both significators are direct and are not about to turn retrograde. If one of the significators turns retrograde within a week, for example, then the party it signifies will withdraw or have a change of mind and so unsettle the whole arrangement.

• Whether or not Mercury is retrograde or in hard aspect with Neptune. Mercury is the significator of contracts, and the chance of a contract being broken or modified is greater when this planet is retrograde than when it is direct. With hard aspects to Mercury, all sorts of errors (not necessarily willful) can be present in the contract and all sorts of important papers can go astray. Misunderstandings are more likely to occur during negotiations also.

• Whether Saturn is well placed. A well-placed Saturn is always helpful where official bodies are concerned. But if Saturn is badly placed there is a big chance of obstacles arising from state laws and taxes.

• Whether further aspects of the Moon before it leaves the sign might indicate unpleasant developments.

In an event chart, we need to bear in mind that the party making the proposal to form a business partnership falls in the 1st house and that the party to whom the proposal is made falls in the 7th. The other rules remain the same.

Now let us take a look at Chart 19 on page 172. It refers to a question put by a man who wanted to set up in business and had his eye on a woman he considered very capable, whom he hoped to

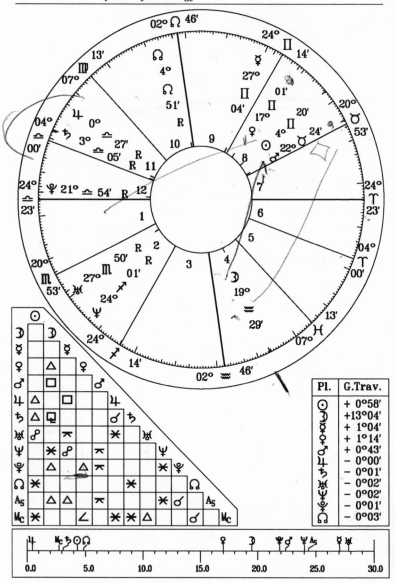

Chart 19. Will I hire this person? Amsterdam, Holland (52 N 22, 4 E 54), May 25, 1981, 3:48 P.M. GMT. Placidus houses. Chart calculated by Astrolabe using *Nova Printwheels*.

employ or to take into partnership. He wanted to know how this would turn out.

The man, himself, is symbolized by Venus and the Moon; the woman is the other party. If employed, she will fall in the 6th house and her significator will be Mars. If taken on as a partner, she will fall in the 7th house and, as it happens, her ruler will still be Mars. Therefore a single analysis will cover both eventualities.

There is no aspect, even in the near future, between Venus and Mars, and even less is there any question of planetary reception. The Moon is the querent's other significator, and is in the process of forming a square to Mars. This can point to misunderstandings, difficulties, and differences of opinion. What is more, Mars is not particularly well placed in Taurus. Mercury's indications are negative, too. Before leaving his sign, he makes no further aspect. What is more, he has just left an opposition to Neptune, which may imply that there has already been some hazy thinking and muddled planning over the matter. The last aspect made by the Moon before it leaves the sign is a square to Uranus. Now, at one stroke, this presents us with three warnings: the square to Uranus can, in itself, indicate sudden unpleasant changes; so that the querent regrets what he started or, at least, regrets the way in which he started it. Again, this hard aspect is with a retrograde planet — which can aggravate matters. Finally, Uranus is Lord of 4, and the 4th house has to do with the end of things.

Mars is in the process of making an opposition to Uranus, showing that the other party is going to cause tensions, no matter whether the woman is an employee or becomes a partner. If we want to know how profitable the business would be, we must look at the 11th house (the 2nd from the 10th). Jupiter is posited here, but unfortunately it is retrograde. However, it is not even necessary to examine planets in the house; the house ruler is Mercury, and this has no further major aspect. Consequently, the house ruler can do nothing to help, and the business will have little or no success.

In short, this chart is very unpromising. And although the querent was enthusiastic and started to forge ahead with his plans, he was pulled up short by a change of attitude in the woman. A number of serious points of disagreement arose, and in the end they parted with a quarrel.

Relationships, Marriage and Divorce

Many of the questions put to astrologers relate to marriage or divorce, for which we naturally consult the 7th house. If we follow the rules as they generally apply, most horary charts will present no problems on this score. A marriage is in the cards when the significators of the querent and those of the other party are forming a positive applying aspect. Problems will be looming when there is a negative applying aspect. If there are no applying aspects, it is more than likely that nothing will happen.

Difficult indications are needed if there is to be a divorce: Uranus in the 1st house, the significators of the querent and the partner in a difficult applying aspect, and so on. What also threatens problems or rather critical situations, is the placement of the significators of both parties in signs where they are not at home.

An important role in questions of marriage and divorce is played by a retrograde significator. Here we must carefully examine the facts of the situation. If the question concerns the possibility of marriage, and the significator of the intended partner is retrograde, then, on the grounds of the meaning of a retrograde planet—that it is bad for anything new—we may conclude that there will be no wedding. But experience teaches that things are not always as simple as that. A retrograde planet can mean that the person it represents is still tied to a marriage partner or to a former husband or wife. A "new marriage" for someone like this can mean a return to the old state of matrimony by reconciliation or remarriage. In such a case, a retrograde planet can work very positively.

If the party concerned has never been married, even in the "common law" sense, a retrograde significator may well mean that this party draws back or that other obstacles arise.

If we delineate the question, "Am I going to get divorced?", the retrograde significator represents the party wishing to return to the old situation and to avoid a separation. Often we actually hear this party say, "But can't everything go on as before? Can't we make a fresh start?" If the significator of the querent is retrograde, the latter will take no further steps to obtain a divorce, but turns back. However, if the other party wants a separation while the querent does not, and the querent's significator is retrograde, the querent may certainly wish to return to the old state, but there is no promise that he or she will be successful in this. For when the two indicators are linked by difficult applying aspects, the retrograde party is the loser.

In this day and age, the question, "Shall we marry or just end up living together?" is quite topical. And it is not all that easy to answer by astrology; because the partner, whatever his or her status, falls in the 7th house. For further enlightenment, it is a good idea to turn to the 9th house in relation to houses 1 and 7 (querent and partner). The reason for this is that all sorts of ceremonies, including the marriage ceremony, come within the scope of the 9th house. A good 9th house, connected in some way with one or both of the significators, suggests marriage rather than living together.

Planets in 7 can sometimes provide information on the health of the querent's marriage, and on his or her attitude toward it. If the querent is having problems and if there are further difficulties in the offing, it makes sense to look at houses 1 and 7 for the querent and the partner, at 4 for the ultimate situation for the querent (the 4th house being taken here as representing the end of things), and at the 4th from the 7th, or 10th house of the chart. In the 10th, we see the potential end of the marriage. It should be noted that difficult planets in 10 do not in themselves signify the end of a marriage if the significators are well placed and make a positive applying aspect. Nevertheless, there will certainly be obstacles to overcome.

Chart 20 on page 176 was cast for the moment when an anxious mother told me that her daughter had a man-friend. Her daughter had just been through several trying years and was only recently divorced. The mother wanted to know if the "friendship" would turn out well.

The 1st house in the chart belongs to the mother. Venus is her significator and stands in Aries (the mother's Sun sign was in fact Aries!). Saturn in the 1st house in questions asked out of anxiety always indicates that the anxiety is groundless and that everything will work out fine. So we can start on a positive note.

The daughter falls in the 5th house, and the daughter's friend (there was as yet no talk of marriage or living together) falls in the 5th house from the 5th, that is to say in the 9th house. The daughter's ex-husband, with whom she maintained friendly contact for the sake of their children, falls in the 7th house from the 5th, and thus in the 11th house. (Since the divorce was very recent, time had yet to tell whether the ex-husband would remain one of her circle of friends and so fall in the 11th house, or would become an acquaintance represented by the 3rd house.)

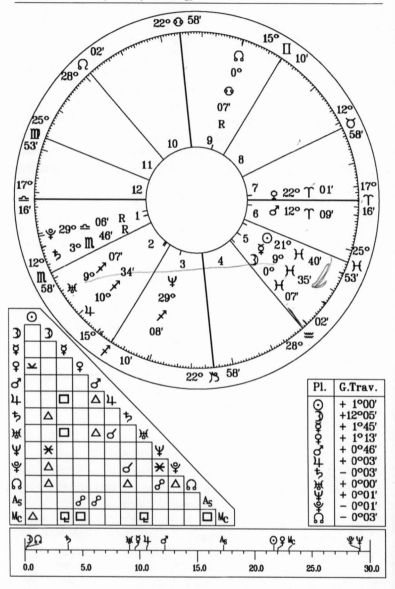

Chart 20. Will my daughter's new relationship turn out well? Amsterdam, Holland (52 N 22, 4 E 54), March 12, 1983, 8:00 P.M. GMT. Placidus houses. Chart calculated by Astrolabe using *Nova Printwheels*.

The daughter's significators are Moon, Mercury, and the Sun as planets in 5, and Saturn, and possibly Uranus, too, as ruler(s) of Aquarius on cusp 5. The 5th house commences in the last degrees of the sign, which is always an indication that changes are on the way for the person concerned—in this case for the daughter.

The significator of the man-friend is Mercury, and that of the ex-husband is the Sun. The Sun and Mercury are also two of her own significators, since they are posited in her own 1st house. This strongly suggests links with both. We must see a warning in the fact that the North Node is the same degree as the Moon, one of the daughter's significators (the Moon is the daughter's ruler of 6, and she met her friend through her work). The North Node can be a sign of good luck, but one always needs to take care whenever it enters into the picture.

Mercury, the significator of the man-friend, has just made a square to Uranus and is on the point of making a full square to Jupiter. If Uranus is accepted as a true significator of the daughter (Aquarius being on cusp 1), this does not throw a very pleasant light on the recent past of the two. It is difficult here to find the right significator of the daughter; she has one or two obvious Uranian traits, but a few strong Saturnian ones as well. She has many planets in Aries and Taurus in her own horoscope (and, interestingly enough, Saturn occupies the 1st house of the horary chart and Uranus occupies the 2nd house!). I thought it best to look at both rulers. And so the applying square between Mercury (the friend) and Uranus (the daughter) becomes highly significant. According to the mother, the daughter was very unsure. Everything had happened too quickly; and, because the new affair had come on the heels of her divorce, she did not know what to do. However, she was very much in love.

Mercury is forming a square to Jupiter. Since the 1st house of her friend is the 5th house of the 5th, the 3rd house of the original chart is the friend's 7th house. The latter is ruled by Jupiter. The man is married, but has already left home once, and is now talking about getting a divorce. The separating square of his significator to Uranus and the applying square of his significator to Jupiter obviously have a bearing on these facts.

The square between Mercury (the friend) and Uranus (the daughter), which has already been exact, is softened by the (also separating) trine between Mercury and her other significator (Saturn). This is a further sign of a positive contact in the past, in spite of the fact that Saturn is retrograde. (The initial approach came from the friend not from her.) A retrograde significator can also point to illness or something of that sort. The woman had suffered for a long time from serious back and leg conditions; and possibly the retrograde motion refers not to her situation but to her state of health. In any case, retrograde Saturn, as her significator, shows that she has let things get on top of her and that her situation is rather precarious.

The Moon has quite a few more aspects to make. First there is a trine to Saturn, which is a positive connection between two of her significators. This may mean that she will become more settled and at rest over her affairs (which turned out to be true). Next comes a square between Mercury and Jupiter: her friend has asked for a divorce in order to make the way free for them both. Then the Moon squares first Uranus and then Jupiter: the situation begins to get out of hand again, she does not know what to do and even wants to stop seeing her friend. After this the Moon makes a conjunction with Mercury: a union of the two of them. Immediately they start living together. Then the Moon is parallel Saturn, split or contraparallel Venus, parallel Mercury, conjunct the Sun, splitparallel Pluto, splitparallel Mars and square Neptune. The last aspect, in particular, is rather troublesome, because it suggests that the relationship will be going through a rather chaotic phase—which is not to say that it will break up. Problems may arise that have to be solved before further progress is made. The one sure thing we can say about Neptune is that it tends to sow confusion.

On looking at the 9th from the 5th house (the 1st house in the chart), which is the daughter's house of ceremonies, we see that it contains Pluto and a retrograde Saturn, not favorable indications for a legal marriage. But Saturn is her significator, which rather alters the case and opens up a possibility, although we may expect her to be slow in making up her mind. The mother declared, after her daughter had set up house with her man-friend, that marriage was not in view, at least for the time being.

If we look at the friend's 9th house, we obtain the 5th house of the chart. And there is his significator, together with that of his lady friend. There are fewer inhibitions here than those shown for her; and in fact, he stated that he was perfectly prepared to marry her after his divorce had come through.

The relationship will therefore hang in the balance to some extent, but much depends on the daughter. For Mercury, as significator of her friend, is weaker in Pisces than her significator Saturn is in

Scorpio. But the retrograde motion of her significator does not speak of an easy inner development. The chart presents the picture of a relationship that will not run smoothly by any means, but is not likely to be broken off either. What it suggests is a need for the relationship to mature, exactly as is suggested by the Moon being in the same degree as the North Node.

Perhaps it is good at this point to make the following remarks. That an aspect lies in the future (like the Moon conjunction with Mercury here) need not mean that interjacent unfavorable aspects will inevitably frustrate matters (aspects such as the Moon square Uranus and Jupiter here). Obviously, the aspects that come along first do, if unfavorable, carry the risk of spoiling things; but a good aspect later on will retain its promise, and I have often seen that promise fulfilled in spite of smaller or larger difficulties in the meantime. Especially in relationships, it is unwise to see a chart as entirely painted in black and white, because mature adults are able to cope with problems without endangering the relationships they value.

Gambling

A question that millions of people ask themselves from time to time is, "I wonder if my lottery ticket will win the big prize?" It is much easier to answer this question than it is to win the prize itself. We must look at the 5th house, which is always the one that tells us about gambling, lotteries and speculation. When the Lord of 5 is well-placed, there is always a chance of winning a prize. By well-placed we mean in an angle and in a sign where it has freedom to act, not retrograde and not aspected by malefics. A favorable applying aspect to or from the Lord of 2 increases the chance; as does a favorable applying aspect to or from the Lord of 8, seeing big money circulating falls in 8.

In Chart 21 on page 180 we see that the significator of the querent and that of the querent's prize ticket is one and the same planet, namely Mercury. This in itself is a very good sign, but there is little hope. Mercury is retrograde, which both weakens the position of the querent and also tells us that the promise will not be fulfilled. A big prize is ruled out. What is more, Mercury is in a cadent house, which is not a helpful indication.

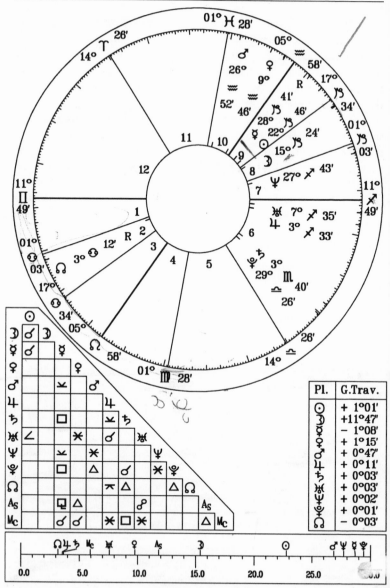

Chart 21. Will I win the big prize? Amsterdam, Holland (52 N 22, 4 E 54), January 13, 1983, 12:44 P.M. GMT. Placidus houses. Chart calculated by Astrolabe using *Nova Printwheels*.

The querent's second significator is the Moon, which is approaching a conjunction with Mercury, but must first encounter the Sun. Because Mercury is retrograde, it is moving toward the Moon, but also meets the Sun first. And the Moon is ruler of 2. Sometimes a third planet assists a matter (see translation and collection of light), but in this instance, the retrograde motion of the planet that is significator of the querent and of the lottery (since it is Lord both of 1 and of 5) is such a negative factor nothing can do much good. Not surprisingly, the querent won nothing.

Travel

One morning, a friend phoned who was about to go on vacation. She had arranged to spend several weeks in a sunny place with her young son and a male friend of the family, but she was anxious about the trip. In the end, she gave me a call to ask whether she ought to go or not, and wanted to know whether her premonition was correct that some sort of trouble was brewing. Should she cancel the holiday, whatever the cost? See Chart 22 on page 182.

She is definitely going on holiday. That much is crystal clear, because Uranus as her first significator (she is an Aquarius) and Jupiter as her second, are both in the 9th house — the house of foreign travel. Before leaving Libra, the Moon is going to form a trine to Mars, a parallel to Pluto, a sextile to Neptune, and a conjunction to Pluto. Mars rules Scorpio and so does Pluto. So the Moon, as significator of the three holiday-makers, is linked by aspect three times with the two rulers of the 9th house (by trine, parallel, and conjunction). This, too, is a very positive indication that they will go and enjoy their visit.

The Moon has already made trines to Venus (ruler of 3) and Mercury (co-ruler of 7 because of Virgo's interception), showing that the plans are already complete.[2] The Moon has also been square to the

---

[2]Some people may question whether or not Venus is also a co-ruler of the 3rd house. Mercury is used as a co-ruler because it is intercepted in the 3rd, a factor that I have discussed earlier. However, even though Libra also has degrees in this house, I do not use it as a co-ruler. I only use the ruler of the sign on the cusp, and the ruler of an intercepted sign, if there is one present.

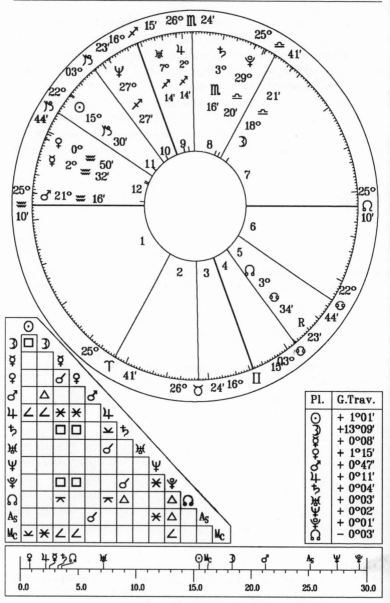

Chart 22. Should I take this vacation? Amsterdam, Holland (52 N 22, 4 E 54), January 6, 1983, 9:39 A.M. GMT. Placidus houses. Chart calculated by Astrolabe using *Nova Printwheels*.

Sun, which reveals that our querent had been worried earlier about whether she should go on vacation or not. One of the reasons was that she was afraid that she might have problems with her traveling-companion, although she could not say why. (Interestingly enough, where journeys are concerned, Mercury in the 12th house of the horary chart, or a retrograde Mercury, is said to show that the querent is reluctant to go traveling. Here we find Mercury in 12.)

It is a little hard to locate the traveling companion in the chart: he is a friend of the family, but the querent regards him more as someone nice to talk to and good to go on holiday with than as an everyday friend. She does not think of him as an acquaintance. People who are difficult to place in a chart fit into the 7th house. The significators of the traveling companion are therefore Mercury, the Sun, and the Moon. The Moon plays a threefold role—it is a significator of the querent, a significator of the traveling companion because it is posited in 7, and a significator of the querent's child because Cancer is on the 5th cusp.

On studying the chart further, we note the fact that Mars is applying to a sextile to Neptune; this is a sextile of the Lord of 9 to one of the querent's significators (Neptune as trans-Saturnian ruler of Pisces). Neptune itself is applying to a sextile with Pluto, and we find here that two trans-Saturnian significators—the querent and foreign travel—are harmoniously linked. But even if we are unwilling to use this aspect because it is not between any of the classical planets, the above-mentioned positive aspects justify us in concluding that the journey will be made and that it will be a success.

Mercury, the significator of the traveling companion, also makes an applying sextile to Uranus, significator of the querent and a planet in 9, which further suggests that the trip will be a happy one. What is more, Mars, the Lord of 9, is making a trine to Pluto (the trans-Saturnian Lord of 9) and a sextile to Neptune (a co-significator of the querent). If we treat Pluto as Lord of 9, we observe that it is void of course, which is an indication that the querent's worries are ill-founded.

However, there are three troublesome little indications. Firstly, the Moon is in the Via Combusta, which is said to be a warning not to try and interpret the chart. But, in my experience, it means only that there is something uncertain, some hard to predict factor in the subject about which the question is asked. Secondly, Saturn is in the same degree as the North Node, and Saturn is the traditional ruler of Aquarius and a significator of this woman. There could be some sort of warning here. Thirdly, Mercury is ruler of 4 and co-ruler of 7. As co-ruler of 7, it could point to disagreements with the traveling companion. But as Mercury makes a separating sextile to Jupiter and an applying sextile to Uranus (both significators of the querent), I did not think that the square presaged any serious discord between the two adults. The square seemed more likely to apply to Mercury in its role as Lord of 4. Problems over accommodation or food during the vacation perhaps?

It was a fine, happy holiday without mutual problems. The only hitch was that, on their arrival at the airport, the travelers learned that their original hotel was fully booked and that they were being transferred elsewhere. However, everything was sorted out with no great inconvenience.

Questions about journeys can also be tackled in another way. In this, we do not take the moment of the question but the moment of departure (or the planned moment of departure). This horary chart has, in addition to the usual rules, a number of points to which we should pay attention. Of course, the first thing to note is whether the journey is short (3rd house) or long (9th house). But we always look at Mercury.

Planets in the 3rd or 9th house can reveal a great deal about the journey. Benefics like Venus and Jupiter promise a pleasant trip, malefics generally warn of an unpleasant one. But if a malefic is strong by sign and is also harmoniously aspected, the journey can turn out to be very important; the malefic lends weight to it in some way or other. In our example, we saw Jupiter in 9 in Sagittarius, an excellent indication of an enjoyable journey.

In the chart of a journey, the 1st house represents the means of transport whatever it is. It is immaterial whether it is our own car, a coach, an airplane or a bicycle. The state and reliability of the conveyance is given by the 1st house. And, as always, when looking at the 1st house, we consider the planets posited in it and the placement of its ruler.

The 4th house has to do with the departure time. I have more than once observed that, with a retrograde Lord of 4, departure was not punctual, perhaps being subject to considerable delay. Where there are hard aspects to the Lord of 4, the trip may even be postponed!

The 7th house represents the areas traversed and the events of the journey itself. Malefics in 7 point to difficulties encountered en route. The nature of these difficulties is signified by the planet concerned: Saturn means stoppages, Neptune means foggy conditions or going astray. Mars indicates accidents and sometimes robbery; but Mercury sometimes points to theft, too. Aspects of the Lord of 7 to these planets have a similar meaning. If we are sailing, the 7th house gives the port of disembarkation.

The 10th house represents the official destination or terminus; also the destination in a metaphorical sense, that is to say, the "fate" of the travelers. With a retrograde Lord of 10, one is not likely to reach one's destination. But if the Lord of 10 is good in other respects, this is probably due to a change of plans on the way; by which one simply chooses another destination, or decides to go wandering around. However, we have to be careful how we apply this rule. One result of mass tourism is that, in the high season of some years, large numbers of holiday-makers either never set out, or go exploring at random.

An important warning is to avoid taking a journey when the chart contains a yod or many inconjuncts, or a Moon in the same degree as the North Node. The traveler(s) will more than likely be dogged by bad luck, and will have to cope with setbacks and difficulties.

Changes made during the journey — for instance, in the ultimate destination — can often be seen in the aspects still to be made by the Moon. An aspect to the Lord of 1, the Lord of 3, a planet in 3 or to Mercury, often represents a change of plan. And if we look at the house in which the Moon is posited, and then move six houses back, we shall find that the changes that take place will turn the house upside down. (Do not ask me how this happens, it is just one of those inexplicable working rules known to astrologers.) For example, the Moon stands in 7. Six houses back we find the 2nd house, so any changes will upset finances.

The planets aspected by the Moon can provide information on the reason for the change and on the way it takes place. Thus, the Sun will not change, Mercury brings about change on account of the weather or of outside influences; Venus for social reasons; Jupiter for the sake of improvement; Saturn on carefully worked-out lines; Uranus in a way that is unexpected or forced; Neptune with concealed premeditation or emotionally; and Pluto to avoid confrontations, troubles, rows and the like.

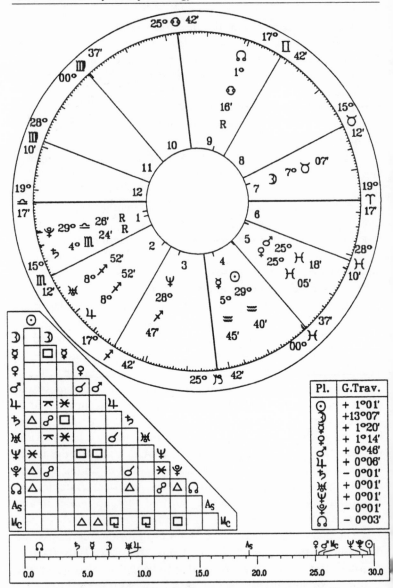

Chart 23. Will the pregnancy and childbirth produce a healthy baby? Amsterdam, Holland (52 N 22, 4 E 54), February 18, 1983, 9:38 P.M. GMT. Placidus houses. Chart calculated by Astrolabe using *Nova Printwheels.*

Pregnancy and Birth

Horary Chart 23 concerns a question asked by a man. A female friend of himself and his wife was pregnant with her first child rather late in life. Although the pregnancy was progressing normally, he was sometimes worried that things might go wrong. He kept asking himself if the confinement would be all right, if the child would be well-formed and healthy, and so on. He knew at the back of his mind that he was probably getting worked up over nothing, but he did it just the same, for he was so fond of this friend, that he wanted only the best for her. Because his anxiety could very well be baseless, he put his question in this form: "How will the rest of the pregnancy and confinement turn out, and is the baby all right?"

Because he asked the question on behalf of a friend, we must treat the 11th house of the chart as if it were the first. The friend's significator is Mercury. Her baby comes in the 3rd house, since that is the 5th from the 11th. The baby's significators are Jupiter, as Lord of the house, and Neptune as the planet in that house. Also we must look at the Moon as a co-significator of the friend.

Mercury is in Aquarius and is forming a sextile to Jupiter; in other words, the significators of the mother and child are about to make a harmonious aspect with one another. This is a significant positive indication, and suggests that the child is healthy and that the mother will be pleased.

According to Rex Bills, all types of birth fall under Pluto and the Sun. Since Pluto in a sign is a generational factor, it is best if we restrict ourselves to the Sun. The latter stands in the last degree of Aquarius and makes no further major aspects before moving into Pisces; in other words, the Sun is void of course, meaning in this case — stop worrying, nothing is going to happen.

A less comforting indication is formed by Neptune being in the baby's house and the fact that its significator, Jupiter, is exactly conjunct Uranus in the 2nd house of the chart. That 2nd house is the 4th from the 11th. So the child will come home. But it is the baby's 12th house, and this points to a stay in hospital where something sudden or unexpected (Uranus) happens. That something of the sort is possible, is also shown by the presence of Neptune in the 5th from the 11th house. The confinement may be attended by complications — but not serious ones, given the placement of the Sun, and the applying sextile between Mercury and Jupiter. What is more, Saturn and Pluto stand in the querent's house, the 1st house, and they are both retrograde. They represent the querent's anxiety; but Saturn's position in 1 and the retrograde motion both show that the anxiety is groundless.

Before leaving Taurus, the Moon is splitparallel Saturn, splitparallel the Sun, sextile Mars, and sextile Venus. Nothing problematical there; and the conclusion, therefore, is that the child will be normal. There is little cause for concern, except that there could be a (small) complication during the confinement. The child was born perfectly healthy. The only unusual feature about the delivery was that it was a vacuum extraction.

Incidentally, it is interesting to note that the querent's significator (because he is represented by the 1st house) is Venus, and Venus is in Pisces, which is his birth sign. The Moon stands in Taurus, and cusp 11 is Virgo. The friend is a Taurus with a Virgo Ascendant.

Legacies

Questions over legacies are very frequent, unfortunately. Even though they may be very difficult from a legal point of view, they are very easy to judge by the horary method. We need to observe the following:

- An inheritance is due when the Lord of the 1st house (the querent) is making a favorable applying aspect to the Lord of the 8th house (the legacy). The same is true of a favorable applying aspect between the Moon and the Lord of 8.

If we are dealing with general family possessions, and if the question is not being asked of one member of the family in particular, then we must look at the 2nd, 4th and 5th houses. For example, the querent may ask something like this, "Can I expect to receive a family inheritance within a fairly short space of time?" without having in mind any member of the family who might be making a bequest. The 2nd house is the possessions of the querent, the 5th house is the 2nd from the 4th and indicates the family possessions. If there is a favorable applying aspect between the two significators of these possessions, or if they are in reception or in each other's houses, or are both aspecting one and the same planet, then there will be an inheritance.

• If we know which member of the family is expected to die, then instead of the 4th and 5th houses, we have to use the houses that represent this member. For brothers and sisters these would be the 3rd and the 2nd from the 3rd, etc. In making our judgment the same rules apply as above.

• A legacy can also present problems; for example, when the debts of the estate are greater than the value of the possessions. When one of the significators makes a hard aspect to Saturn, the danger of this is very great. Even a harmonious aspect to Saturn seems to reduce the worth of the final settlement, through debts, deficiencies, and so on. If Neptune enters the picture, there is a risk of fraud, of a dishonest lawyer, of lost documents (whether or not they have been mislaid intentionally), and so on. Even harmonious aspects to Neptune are dangerous! If the ruler of the house of the possessions of the family member concerned is retrograde, then the inheritance is often less than expected.

• The legacy is large when one of the significators makes a positive aspect with the Sun or with Jupiter.

The following example, Chart 24 on page 190, relates to the question of a man who asked, "Shall I inherit anything from my grandfather?" For a start, we see a restriction placed on interpretation, namely that the Ascendant is in the first degrees of a sign: in other words, it is still too soon to answer this question. But let us examine the chart cautiously, in the light of the foregoing rules. The grandfather can fall in two houses: in the 1st (as 4th from the 10th), or in the 7th (as 4th from the 4th). Since the 1st house always belongs to the querent, I choose the 7th house in such a case as the house of the grandfather, and have found that it works out well in practice. The Sun, as significator of the querent, is in the house representing the grandfather. The grandfather seems to be very fond of this man, and the querent is also fond of his grandfather. The querent is further signified by the Moon. The grandfather is signified by Saturn as Lord of Aquarius, and by the Sun as a planet in 7. Saturn is Lord of 8, too, of the 2nd house from the 7th and thus significator of the grandfather's possessions.

We see no favorable applying aspects between the significators of the querent and Saturn. The significator of the querent's 2nd house is the Sun, and this gives even less positive indications. There is even a

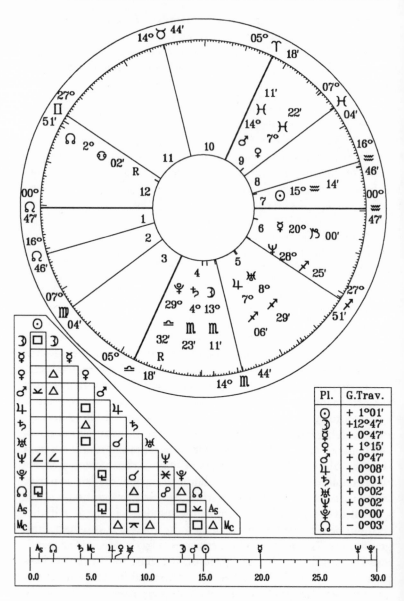

Chart 24. Shall I inherit anything from my grandfather? Amsterdam, Holland (52 N 22, 4 E 54), February 4, 1983, 3:03 P.M. GMT. Placidus houses. Chart calculated by Astrolabe using *Nova Printwheels*.

square imminent between the Moon (significator of the querent) and the Sun (significator of the querent *and* of his grandfather).

So the answer to the question seems to be "no." But there is this to say about it, that it was really still too early to ask, in view of the degree actually on the Ascendant. Not long afterward, the querent heard that his grandfather had still not made a will nor even any dispositions concerning his estate; so the querent was indeed making his inquiry too soon.

When a will does, in fact, exist, we must look to see whether Mercury, or the ruler of the financial house of the family member, is retrograde. In that case, an alteration is going to be made in the will. Whether this alteration will be to the advantage or disadvantage of the querent depends on the aspects to the significators of the latter.

Worrying Situations

Sometimes there are questions about the end of life. Such questions touch on an ethically dubious and fiercely controversial side of astrology—death prediction. Naturally, in horary astrology, ethics are a most important consideration, and we should always be very wary of predicting death. People's motives for asking this type of question about a person or animal can be bad as well as good; they may be actuated by malice as well as by genuine care.

A mistake here on the part of the astrologer can do incalculable harm, irrespective of the accuracy of the forecast. Even if the individual does not die, the prediction can set dangerous psychic processes in motion. The querent can try to steel himself or herself against the supposed blow; perhaps by becoming less attached, so that the separation will not be felt so keenly when it comes. Then, if the loved one does not die, the relationship will never return to quite the same footing—something has crept in to spoil it. Again, the querent may tend to panic at every telephone call, every slight sound or cough; and this hardly contributes to a helpful atmosphere. Of course, it would be utterly wrong to tell the patient that, according to the chart, time is running out. "Hope cherishes life" as the old saying goes. By passing an astrological "death sentence," we strike at the root of that hope and side with the destructive forces against the forces working for the person's recovery.

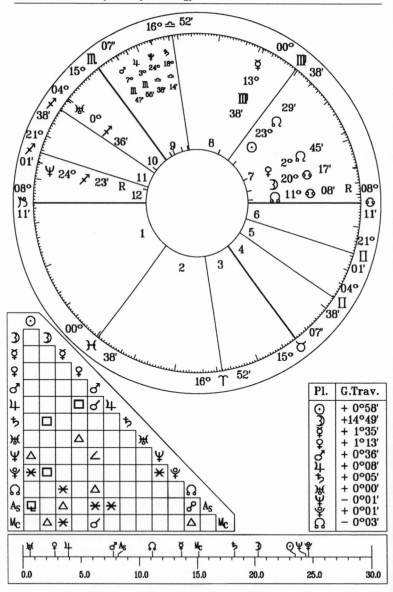

Chart 25. Event chart of a seriously ill kitten going to the vet. Amsterdam, Holland (52 N 22, 4 E 54), August 16, 1982, 4:52 P.M. GMT. Placidus houses. Chart calculated by Astrolabe using *Nova Printwheels*.

As astrologers, not only should we be extremely careful over how we manage questions of life and death, we should make it a rule never to predict certain death. The price the querent would have to pay for such knowledge is far too high. Therefore I have debated with myself for a long time over whether I should deal with the subject at all. Two things have finally persuaded me to do so. In the first place, there are many astrological practitioners who, at some time or another, are tempted to use their art to answer a question concerning death for their own interest by means of a horary chart. I have often observed that their anxiety has led them to make mistakes in interpretation, which has made matters worse. In the second place, we are sometimes asked whether or not a sick pet will recover. To try and obviate errors of interpretation in such delicate matters where fear and stress are involved, I shall discuss some relevant examples.

Sometimes there is a limitation on judgment in the chart of a question concerning whether a certain person will live or die, the "figure is not radical" as we say. In this case, *do not*, I repeat *not*, go any further with this chart! There is not sufficient material for making a reliable assessment.

Consider, for example, Chart 25. It is an event horoscope, the chart of the moment a married couple brought their sick kitten into the consulting room of a veterinary surgeon. The kitten was examined every week because it was very ill. There had been no sign of improvement and, in the consulting room, the kitten suffered an attack of what looked like epilepsy. After more tests, the veterinarian decided that the little creature was only going to get worse, that it was blind and suffering pain. He also said that the epileptic fits would increase in frequency until the animal died of them. The owners could not make up their minds what to do and wanted further advice. They were hoping against hope for an improvement and were prepared to do everything that lay in their power to help their pet.

The horary chart provides the following information. In an event horoscope, the party taking the initiative — in this case the married couple — is indicated by the first house. Their kitten falls in the 5th house. The significators of the married couple are Saturn, and possibly Uranus for the intercepted sign Aquarius in 1 — if we allow modern rulerships. Mercury is the kitten's significator. To see what the kitten's prospects are, we treat the 5th house as if it were the 1st and note that this puts Mercury in the new 4th. This is not encouraging, because one of the meanings of the 4th house is the end of things. Certainly,

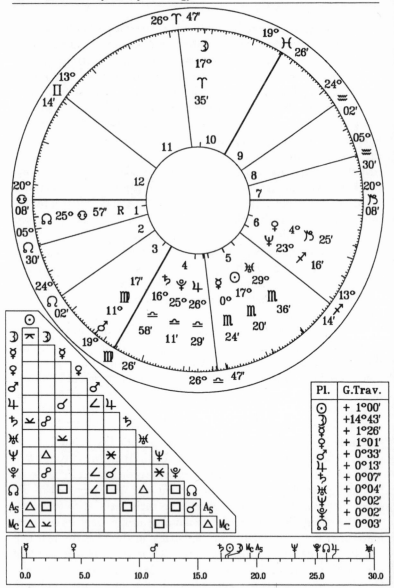

Chart 26. Event chart of a friend, telling about her son's accident. Amsterdam, Holland (52 N 22, 4 E 54), November 9, 1981, 7:46 P.M. GMT. Placidus houses. Chart calculated by Astrolabe using *Nova Printwheels*.

Mercury is strong in Virgo, but the only aspect it makes from that sign into the far future is a square to Neptune—which is not favorable, either. However, before this square to Neptune, Mercury forms a parallel with Pluto and a parallel with Saturn. In itself, the parallel with Saturn could mean that the owners and the pet would be reunited, but this ray of hope has a shadow cast over it by the last, unfavorable aspect to Mercury, made especially ominous by the fact that Neptune is retrograde. The Moon is strong in Cancer. Before leaving Cancer, it makes a square to Pluto and a contraparallel to Neptune, both of which are unfavorable indications. In particular, the parallel to Neptune can be dangerous here, because Neptune is posited in the kitten's 8th house (the 12th is the 8th from the 5th) and therefore has a direct bearing on the life and death of the animal.

Thus both Mercury and the Moon make their last aspects with this planet, which is very unfortunate. What is more, Venus, the kitten's Lord of 12, is approaching a square to Jupiter, the kitten's Lord of 8. All these indications are negative, and there seems to be little further hope for the animal.

Even before I expressed this opinion as cautiously as possible to the owners, they had already decided to have their pet put to sleep. It died before the whole of the fatal dose was given.

The next example, Chart 26, is again an event horoscope, cast for the moment when a good friend phoned me in a panic. Her 9 year old son had been rushed into hospital and was lying in Intensive Care. He had been hit by a speeding car, had been hurled a distance of seven-and-a-half yards, and had landed on his head. She was scared stiff that he would not recover, or would suffer from permanent, severe injuries.

The mother's significator is the Moon, because Cancer is on the Ascendant (her Sun sign is also Cancer). The child has several significators: Venus as ruler of Libra on cusp 5; also Jupiter, Mercury, the Sun and Uranus, all crowded into the 5th house. If the 5th house is treated as the 1st, we see a Pluto/Jupiter conjunction on the child's Ascendant.

To discover whether death will result, we always have to look at planets in 8 and 12, as the Lords of 8 and 12, and to some extent at the 4th house. Mercury is ruler of the child's 8th and 12th houses, and stands in his 1st house—an unprepossessing indication. But Venus, as significator of the child, and Mercury, are shortly going to form a

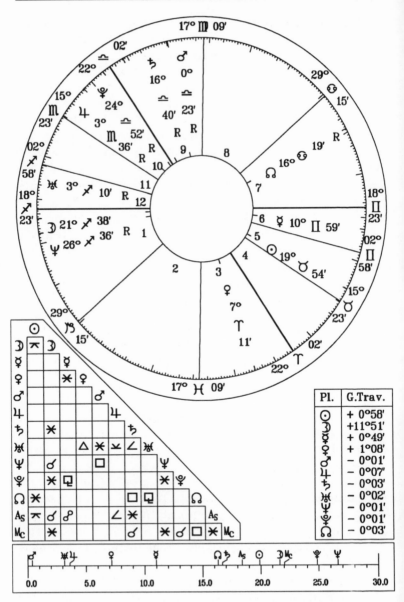

Chart 27. Will my daughter come through the operation? Leyden, Holland (52 N 09, 4 E 30), May 10, 1982, 9:50 P.M. GMT. Placidus houses. Chart calculated by Astrolabe using *Nova Printwheels.*

sextile to one another without any other aspect intervening, and that is a marvellous indication that things may be expected to turn out well.

According to Rex Bills, the brain is ruled by Mercury, Aries and the Moon; and between brackets he mentions houses 1 and 3, and the Sun. We note that the Moon is in Aries in the child's 6th house, and the Moon has just made an opposition to Saturn, the ruler of the child's 3rd house. This separating opposition points to a traumatic situation in the recent past: the child seems to have been severely concussed. Mercury, however, does not aggravate this indication; on the contrary, we saw that this planet points to a development in a positive direction. Yet, Saturn as Lord of 3 is posited in 12, a sign that something is amiss.

The aspects still to be made by the Moon are the following: trine to Neptune, split-parallel to Saturn, opposition to Pluto, opposition to Jupiter and parallel to Pluto. The last aspect is a parallel, and Pluto is the trans-Saturnian Lord of Scorpio and therefore co-ruler of the child's 1st house, which may be regarded as a positive sign. There will be relapses as well as improvements, but the picture on the whole does not show a fatal prognosis. Saturn, Pluto, Jupiter, and Mercury stand in the Via Combusta but, at the most, this should mean either that the chart presents a slightly more serious state of affairs than would otherwise appear, although certainly not too serious, or that the extent and duration of the injuries can not immediately be determined.

Permanent damage is not apparent: the ruler of the child's 6th house (the 10th in the chart) is Jupiter, and Jupiter makes no further major aspect from the sign in which it is posited. Thus we do not need to become over-anxious. However, Pluto is in the same degree as the North Node—a warning that the collision was a big one.

The accident occurred on November 9, 1981. On November 17, Venus made a full sextile to Mercury at almost 12° Scorpio, and it is a noteworthy fact that eight days after the accident, the child suddenly started to make progress and, from that time onward, could be taken off the life-support system. He did recover.

Horary Chart 27 was cast for the question asked by a mother, herself an astrologer, about her child: "How will my daughter get on in her operation tomorrow? Will she come through it all right?" On February 11, 1981, she had given birth to a baby girl who seemed to have a serious heart defect. The doctor told her that the little girl would have to undergo a major operation in the near future, and that it was not certain that this would be a success. For a while everything went well, but in the spring of 1982 the child's condition deteriorated so rapidly that an operation was required. This was scheduled for May 11th. On the eve of the operation, the above question arose in the mother's mind so clearly that she made a horary chart for it.

In this chart, the mother is signified by Jupiter as Lord of Sagittarius, the Moon, and Neptune. Jupiter is retrograde: the mother herself can do nothing to influence the situation and has to wait passively. Neptune in her 1st house is a bad sign. It always suggests that something will not happen as planned, and may even go wrong. But let us look further. Her small daughter falls in the 5th house and is indicated by Venus as ruler of Taurus and by the Sun as a planet in 5. Venus is in its detriment in Aries and the Sun is peregrine in Taurus, thus neither of the indicators of the child are strongly placed.

Astrologically, the child's heart lies in the 5th house from the 5th, that is in the 9th house of the chart. There we find Saturn and Mars, the two malefics, both retrograde. This is another unpleasant indication. Above all, retrograde Mars is a problem, because it is an ominous sign for an operation. And the planet is in its detriment in Libra. The following day, that is to say during surgery, it was going to become stationary before turning direct. This, too, is a disturbing event. Mars rules the child's 12th house of hospitals and hospitalization, an indication that there is little the hospital can do. Some astrologers assign the role of the anesthetist and everything involving narcosis to the 12th house. A retrograde ruler of that house does not necessarily point to complications or faults in the giving of the anesthetic (although it can sometimes do so). It can also point to spontaneous complications.

We must also study the 8th house, by which I mean the 8th house of the child. Here we find Uranus retrograde, a warning of sudden difficulties. The Lord of 8 is Jupiter, this is retrograde, too. A retrograde planet usually fails to make good its promise, and this may well retrieve a critical situation. So, here a retrograde Lord of 8 would have been reassuring if only it had not been posited with a retrograde Pluto in the child's 6th house; which is anything but a good indication of recovery. Saturn is in the same degree as the North Node, and this is another warning. And Saturn is a planet in the house representing the child's heart, the 5th from the 5th.

Neither Jupiter nor Mars form further major aspects, and are therefore rather isolated. The keyword "nothing" is applicable. But that means that they can do nothing positive for the matter, even if we discount the fact that they are retrograde. Again, the picture is not good.

The Sun, co-indicator of the 4th house of the little girl, stands in the child's 1st house. As ruler of the end of things it is not very propitious there. The Sun has no further major aspects to make from Taurus. The Sun, too, represents the heart, and the fact that it is proceeding on its way alone is hardly encouraging.

The actual ruler of the child's heart, thus the ruler of the 5th house from the 5th, is Mercury. It is essentially fortified in Gemini, so the placement is excellent. But the last aspect it will make in that sign is an opposition to retrograde Neptune — which speaks for itself. After the conjunction with Neptune, the Moon finally makes a parallel with Neptune. A parallel is a connection, but Neptune has no immediate reference to the operation, so this connection can not contribute to a positive outcome.

Jupiter, Neptune and the Moon, the three significators of the mother, are not joined in the near future by applying aspect to the two significators of the child, namely Venus and the Sun. If we take into consideration this lack of a connection between mother and child in the near future and combine this (in itself less important) fact with all the previous indications, we are forced to acknowledge that the situation is very grave. Perhaps the retrograde significators of 8 and 12 can offer some relief, but this is a very slim chance. They could have a delaying effect.

The operation was an extremely difficult one and lasted a whole day. Next day the little girl was in great danger, but improved after receiving large doses of medication. However, the improvement lasted only a few days. On May 23, the child died, after being in a very bad way for a while. The mother said that the death was thought to be due to poisoning or to an attack of meningitis (remember the last two aspects of the Moon — a conjunction with and parallel to Neptune).

The progressions of mother and child would have confirmed the anxious suspicions aroused by the horary chart, although death as such can never be predicted by a progression. See Charts 28 and 29 (pages 200, 201). The mother's progressions around the birth of her child on February 11, 1981 were:

Primary:
Moon trine MC, exact on June 15, 1981;
Moon square Pluto, exact November 14, 1981;

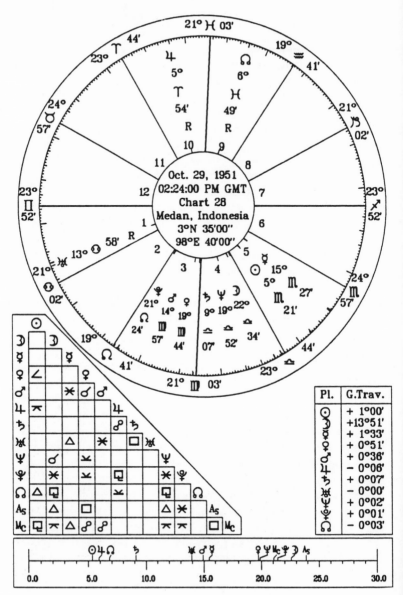

Chart 28. The mother's natal chart. Medan, Indonesia (3 N 35, 98 E 40), October 29, 1951, 2:24 P.M. GMT. Placidus houses. Chart calculated by Astrolabe using *Nova Printwheels*.

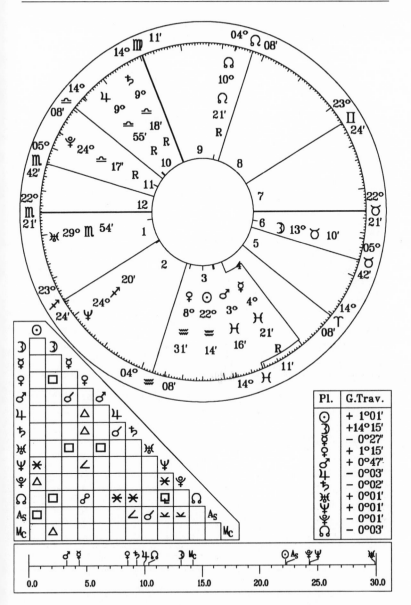

Chart 29. The baby's natal chart. Amsterdam, Holland (52 N 22, 4 E 54), February 11, 1981, · 1:18 A.M. GMT. Placidus houses. Chart calculated by Astrolabe using *Nova Printwheels*.

Venus conjunct Neptune, exact on October 4, 1981;
Jupiter opposition Sun, full on July 2, 1981.

Secondary:
Moon trine MC, exact April 2, 1981;
Moon square Pluto, exact April 11, 1981.

Transits (orb 1°):
Neptune opposite Ascendant;
Venus trine Saturn;
Sun trine Ascendant, trine Moon, opposite Pluto;
Jupiter and Saturn conjunct Saturn;
Moon sextile Uranus.

As we know, primary directions last a long time; they often color the
events for more than a year, although they seem on the whole to be
strongest during the months before the exact date (seldom anything
happens on the date itself!). The Moon trine MC is a beautiful indication of motherhood. However, in progressions we must always bear in
mind that the pattern in the birth chart plays a part. And here we find
a Moon inconjunct the MC (150°). The difficulties of such an inconjunct keep rising to the surface with renewed progressive contact
between these two points. In the birth chart, the Moon and Pluto were
sextile, which is more satisfactory, but they are now square one
another. The sextile should mitigate the square; but here caution is
required!

What we have is a so-called yod aspect—two inconjunct aspects to
one point (in this case, the Moon and Pluto both inconjunct the MC)
with a sextile forming the base of the triangle (in this case, the Moon
sextile Pluto). A yod has a dramatic effect when activated by progressions, and produces a big revolution in the life and outlook of the
person concerned; usually he or she is assailed by difficulties and
stresses. At the time of the birth, the yod in our example chart was
activated by several aspects by primary direction. With such an activation, events sometimes occur that make one think one has been "star-
crossed." This ill-starred time brought a baby into the world with a
cardiac defect.

The Lord of 5 is Venus, and Venus will be conjunct primary
directed Neptune, an aspect becoming exact later in the year. Jupiter's
opposition to the Sun is important, too: the Sun posited in 5 also rules

children. The opposition of Jupiter is made even more ominous by the fact that Jupiter and the Sun are already inconjunct in the radix.

Extra emphasis is laid on the yod in the secondary progressions. And, in the transits, we see Neptune's opposition to the Ascendant as another of the difficult indications. Now note, we must never jump to conclusions and predict on the basis of these progressions that "something is bound to go wrong with the child the native is carrying." There are so many other ways in which the progressions can work out that to attempt such a precise forecast is not only to attempt the impossible, but also to do something very unethical. But, on looking at the progressions after the event, they do not seem inappropriate in the mother's case. She had to meet any problems in the year after the confinement, and experience much sorrow.

She had the following progressions around the time of her baby daughter's death on May 23, 1982:

Primary:
Midheaven trine Pluto, exact January 8, 1982;
Ascendant sextile Venus, exact February 21, 1982;
Ascendant square Neptune, exact April 16, 1982;
Venus inconjunct MC, exact November 18, 1982;
Neptune sextile Venus, exact October 10, 1982;
Pluto opposition MC, exact March 6, 1982.

Secondary:
Sun trine Jupiter, exact March 3, 1982;
Venus conjunct Neptune, exact February 15, 1982;
Moon square North Node, exact April 27, 1982.

Transits (orb 1°):
Mercury square Mars;
Venus opposition Moon;
True North Node conjunct Uranus.

Thus, in the primary progressions we see a continuous activation of the yod by the MC trine Pluto, but much more powerfully by Pluto, which itself had formed an opposition to the MC. This is, apart from anything else, a severe crisis-aspect which sometimes goes together with the experience of an emotionally trying situation; even with a bereavement.

The Ascendant is sextile Venus, the ruler of 5. In the birth chart, however, they form a square, which is now brought into play by the harmonious aspect. By secondary progression, Venus is conjunct Neptune. The Sun, which by secondary progression makes an ordinarily much-prized trine to Jupiter, makes an inconjunct to Jupiter in the radix. Now this unfortunate background influence is brought to the fore by the progression, so that the trine is given a more unhelpful significance. Accordingly, there are several very hard aspects around the birth and death of the baby girl of this lady, especially those to do with the yod. In the light of these aspects, the horary chart considered earlier offers little hope.

In the baby's chart (Chart 29 on page 201), Mercury and Mars are conjunct but form no other major aspects. Mercury is Lord of 8 and Mars is Lord of 5 — the heart! Young as the child was, this conjunction played an important part in the progressions. Transiting Uranus made a square to Mars; by primary direction, Mars made its conjunction with Mercury exactly on February 27, 1982; and, by secondary progression, Mercury was steadily approaching Mars by retrograde motion, and was due to make the conjunction exactly on June 30th. These difficult indications all related to the child's rulers of 5 and 8 — the houses of the heart and death respectively; in other words, they highlighted exactly where the trouble lay.

It goes without saying that much more could be said about the progressions and transits. What matters here is that we see how progressions and horary charts always seem to match one another and to provide the same information — as I have already noted. Look, for example, at the yod in the horoscope of this mother. The planets involved are the Moon-Neptune conjunction, sextile Pluto with both ends of the sextile inconjunct the MC. Turning to the horary chart, we see that a yod is formed there by the Sun with the MC and the Moon/Ascendant conjunction. But the Moon is flanked by Neptune and the MC by Pluto, which are therefore indirectly involved in this yod complex. These are the planets that are so unmistakably implicated in the problem, according to the mother's birth chart.

12

Election
Charts

An election chart is a horoscope of a predetermined point in time, selected as being the most favorable possible moment for a certain undertaking. To accomplish this, the astrologer looks for the planetary positions most helpful for the purpose at hand. The astrologer then tries to discover the best time of day for the undertaking. Casting an election chart can be tackled in one of two ways. In the first, we simply rely on the ephemeris for finding the most favorable day and time of day; in the second, we start with the birth chart and use it as our point of departure for finding the best date and time. The most practical method is the following:

• Take the radical house appropriate to the matter in hand. In sickness, for example, this is the 6th house. Now take the cusp of that house and make it the Ascendant of the chart. Next, search the ephemeris for a suitable day. Possibly the required Ascendant is completely impossible for the time of year in question. For instance, it may be quite impractical to find a surgeon who will operate in the wee hours of the morning—at 4:37 A.M.—even though our radical 6th house cusp is on the Ascendant at that time. However, an election chart where the Ascendant makes a harmonious aspect with the radical MC is just as good. It is also good, according to the rules of election

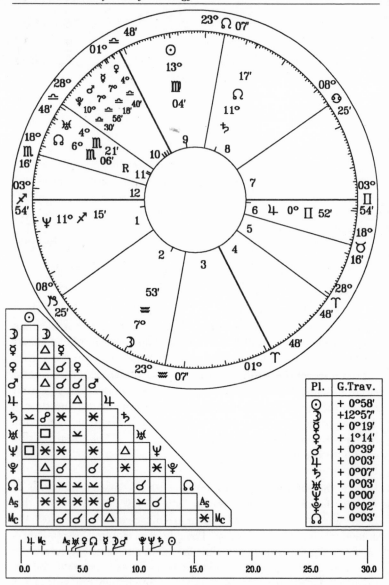

Chart 30. Electional chart of the time to begin working together. Amsterdam, Holland (52 N 22, 4 E 54), September 5, 1976, 12:48 P.M. GMT. Placidus houses. Chart calculated by Astrolabe using *Nova Printwheels*.

horoscopy when the Sun is in the 10th or 11th house, or in the house of the quesited.

• Having determined the degree on the Ascendant in this manner, we can then look up the corresponding MC in a table of houses and calculate the time of day in order to put the planets in the right places.

Usually it is a real challenge to work out an optimum day and time. The question is whether it is worth the trouble. In the first place, an election demands that we recognize *every* astrological influence and system (something that is actually impossible to do, given the tremendous variety in astrology), and also that we have a complete knowledge of these systems and influences and possess an ability to handle them faultlessly. We must also possess a high degree of objectivity. The last requirement is harder to meet than we may think, for why are we trying to erect an election chart anyway? The difficulty in being objective is especially felt in anxiety-producing situations or whenever there is a need for a life-line. These of course are situations where we are personally involved, situations where — with the strongest self-control in the world — we can no longer be genuinely objective. Fear is generally a poor adviser.

If we add the fact that many astrological practitioners (and not all of them beginners) are nervous about malefic effects of Saturn, Uranus, Neptune and Pluto, then it can be a long search before a day and time are found when these planets are showing the more mild sides of their nature. And, when this search is successful, there will surely be something else in the chart to cause problems; something we have completely overlooked in our fixation about the so-called bad planets, but something that will nevertheless inevitably have an effect. A 100 per cent favorable date and time simply does not exist. This means that we have to decide what our priorities are when we cast the election horoscope. If these are prompted by worry, they may not really be suitable for this sort of astrology.

Chart 30 is an election horoscope prepared by astrologer "A" who wished to work on a certain project with astrologer "B." The idea was that they would collaborate for a fairly long time. The astrologer who cast the horoscope was anxious to place Jupiter on the Descendant, because it was the "greater benefic" and he thought it would promote the association. Also, if at all possible, he wanted Jupiter to have various easy aspects; but he did not want Saturn, Neptune, and Pluto to be making hard aspects to the Ascendant and MC, since these are important outlets in the chart. Uranus needed careful placement, too, because it symbolizes astrology. And so, "A" searched and pondered until he discovered what, in his opinion, was the optimum day and time. He then phoned "B" to announce the moment of his arrival on the latter's doorstep. They would start their planned activities at this precisely predetermined moment.

There was "A" standing on the doorstep in time for the two astrologers to start discussing their project at the "right" minute. But they had hardly started when the bell rang. Friends of "B" had unexpectedly arrived, and they interrupted the discussions for a while. Eventually, the talks were resumed and some further appointments were made, and then nothing more happened; "B" has not heard from "A" again, and still can not understand what went wrong.

Now let us look at the chart. Jupiter is indeed on the Descendant, but it is in its detriment in Gemini. What is more, it has barely left the 6th house, which is not a strong house for this planet. As it happens, Jupiter is very influential in the chart, because it is Lord of 1 (and therefore the significator of "A," the party who took the initiative). Thus its placement is already a weak point. Because "A" was determined to have Jupiter on the Descendant at all costs, he had to have Neptune in the 1st house as part of the bargain; and, with Neptune in 1, things never go as planned and there is a danger that they will be allowed to drift. Here we see an "unconsciously chosen danger" brought about by the conscious choice of some other planetary position.

In fact, Jupiter is forming some fine aspects, but its difficult placement makes it next to impossible for much to be made of them. The Moon, too, makes a number of splendid aspects, but some of these have already been exact. There is still an applying trine to Mars (very quick) and one to Pluto, but also an applying opposition to Saturn. And the latter represents a danger for the collaboration. It would have been preferable to have started earlier with more applying aspects of the Moon; but then, of course, Jupiter would not have been on the Descendant. So there was a choice: Jupiter on the Descendant or the Moon with more applying aspects. Personally, I would rather have had the latter.

Apparently the maker of the election overlooked a few very difficult placements at this time and date. The Lord of 7, Mercury, is making an applying conjunction with Mars, a serious warning of discord! And then Mercury is due to make a conjunction with Pluto, Lord of 12 in the chart. This, too, is a far from ideal indication for a good collaboration.

Now take a look at Mercury and the Moon: their next aspects are respectively a conjunction with and a trine to Mars. If we consider the second astrologer, "B," with whom "A" wished to collaborate, and place him in the 7th house, we see that Mars is "B's" ruler of 10 and 11. The applying harmonious aspects between the significator of this astrologer and the significator of his friends (11th house) reflect the visit "B's" friends made almost immediately after the start of his discussion with "A." It is there sure enough, in the election horoscope, but the latter's maker can hardly be blamed for missing it.

Although there is much more that might be said about this chart, I hope that enough has been brought to readers' attention to show that there are numerous facets we can miss when erecting an election horoscope, and that the choices with which we are faced are not simple. If we allow ourselves to become obsessed with a single aim, the great difficulties present elsewhere in the chart can become obscured. No wonder election horoscopes have become so controversial that many astrologers have washed their hands of them.

A point we are quite likely to overlook, in our eagerness to select an auspicious moment, is: "What is the true beginning of a thing?" Is it really the first action, or is it when we start planning, or is it some other moment? Certainly, we can cast an election horoscope for the start of some activity or other, but we will have already given considerable thought to this activity. Is it to be believed that the moment when we were inspired with the idea for the activity is of no importance? In the light of my own experience, I can confidently state that the moment an idea flashed through our minds supplies an important horary chart, and one that is very useful for determining times according to the rules of horary astrology, and for studying with transits and progressions. The later chart of the actual, external start of the matter in question also proves very useful; but the two charts together give the most help. Now the moment of the first "happy thought" is completely outside our control. And what about the moment we actively start to erect an election horoscope: is this not the moment when we start to take external action on our idea?

As a final critical marginal note on elections, let me say this. We bear the full responsibility for something that we have consciously chosen. There is a fair chance that an election will produce disappointments. There are no ideal charts, because a horary chart or an election horoscope can never cancel what stands in the natal chart. The form taken by the disappointment can be read (sometimes only after the event) in the election horoscope itself. But we have brought it upon ourselves by choosing that particular moment. In very important matters, this may be harder to bear than we may think. For what are we going to do, if some essential points go wrong?

An election chart is often a source of hope, however, even if it does no more than foster the illusion that one can guide one's life with it. Sad to say, life does not allow itself to be forced into a pattern in this manner. What will come will come, in one way or another, whatever we try to do about it. The hope gained from an election is delusive: if it convinces us we have certain qualities in ourselves that we do not really possess, a marvellous election is not going to see us through a job interview successfully. We must be realistic. In my experience, things happen at the strikingly right moment — astrologically seen of course (see also chapters 9 and 10). If a situation is good, a bad election or horary chart can not essentially make it worse; all it can do is to hold things up a little. On the other hand, if a situation is bad, a good election will not genuinely improve it, no matter how optimistic we may be.

Nevertheless, if readers wish to experiment with election astrology in spite of all I have said, observe the ordinary rules of horary astrology — these apply to electional astrology, too. Pay attention to the limitations on interpretation, and watch for harmonious applying aspects between the significators of the querent and the quesited. See to it that the Moon is placed as harmoniously as possible and that the significators of the querent and the quesited are not in their debilities (signs where they are weak), and that they are certainly not retrograde. A retrograde Mars and Mercury are also to be avoided. Try to have the planets in their own houses, as far as possible, and free from hard aspects. See if it's possible to get a "good" planet, such as the Sun or Jupiter, in the house of the quesited (or in aspect with the ruler of this house). Avoid having Saturn, Uranus, or Neptune in the 1st house, also the North Node; and make sure that no significator is in the same degree as the North Node. If swift action is desired, then there must not be too many planets in fixed signs — and certainly not the Ascendant or the Moon — or we shall have delays or a slowing of the pace of events. However, in many cases this can lead to a more solid development. Those who use the Part of Fortune should make sure that it is not in Scorpio or Pisces or in the 8th or 12th houses. And for those who work with fixed stars: avoid having the Ascendant, the Moon, and the significators in aspect to a difficult fixed star.

Naturally, there are many more things to avoid according to the rules; but the above make so many demands that I have yet to see the electional horoscope that fulfills them all. Therefore, all I can say to the reader is, "Don't rush into electional astrology blindly; it has far too many snags." For my own part, I do very well without elections.

In Horary astrology the usual information is needed, the date, place and moment of the event or enquiry, the moment of birth of the question

Bibliography

Bills, R. E. *The Rulership Book: A Directory of Astrological Corre-spondences*. Tempe, AZ: The American Federation of Astrologers, 1991.

Brandler-Pracht, K. *Die Stunden-astrologie: Die Lehre von den astrologischen Elektionen*. Leipzig: Astrologische Bibliothek Band VI, Astrologisches Verlagshaus, nd.

Dariott, C. *Dariotus Redivivus; Or a Brief Introduction Conducing to the Judgement of the Stars, wherein the whole Art of Judiciall Astrologie is briefly and plainly delivered; By which a determinate Judgement may be given upon any Question demanded*. London: For Andrew Kemb, 1653.

DeLong, S. *The Art of Horary Astrology in Practice*. With 101 charts. Tempe, AZ: The American Federation of Astrologers, 1980.

————. *Guideposts to Mystical and Mundane Interpretations*. Tempe, AZ: The American Federation of Astrologers, 1980.

DeLuce, Robert. *Horary Astrology*. New York: ASI, 1978.

Gadbury, J. *Genethlialogia. Or the Doctrine of Nativities, containing the whole art of Directions, and Annual Revolutions, Together with the Doctrine of Horarie Questions*. London: Printed for William Miller, 1661–1658.

Goldstein-Jacobson, Ivy M. *Simplified Horary Astrology with Requisite Mathematics*. Alhambra, CA: Frank Severy Publications, 1975.

Jones, M. E. *Horary Astrology: The Technique of Immediacies*. With a Primer of Symbolism. Boston and London: Shambhala, 1975.

Knapp, E. M. *Horary Art and Its Synthesis*. Santa Barbara, CA: Sandollar Press, nd.

Knappich, W. *Geschichte der Astrologie*. Frankfurt am Main, Germany: V. Klostermann, 1967.

Knegt, L. *Uurhoek- en Vragenastroogie. Eeen Practisch Systeem voor de oplossing van Levensvraagstukken*. Amsterdam: Uitverij Schors, nd.

Lehman, Lee, J. *The Book of Rulerships*. West Chester, PA: Whitford Press, 1992.

Leo, Allen. *Horary Astrology: How to Obtain an Answer to any Question (with full glossary of astrological terms)*. London: L. N. Fowler, Astrological Manual Number 7, nd.

Lilly, W. *An Introduction to Astrology: With numerous Emendations, Adapted to the Improved State of the Science*. Hollywood, CA: Newcastle, 1972.

Meyer, M. R. *The Astrology of Change: Horary Astrology and its Humanistic Applications*. New York: Anchor Press, 1975.

Pearce, A. J. *The Textbook of Astrology*. Tempe, AZ: The American Federation of Astrologers, 1970.

Placidus de Titus, D. *Astronomy and Elementary Philosophy, translated from the Latin by E. Sibly, to which are added Introductory Notes and Observations, with a Concise Method of Judging Horary Questions*. London: W. Justins, 1789.

Ram, Th. J. J. *Aktuele Astrologie*. Syllabus van de wintercursus gegevern te Arnhem, 1939–1940.

Raphael. *Uurhoek Astrologie. Waardoor men iedere vraag in verband met de toekomst kan beantwoorden*. Amsterdam: Gnosis, 1931.

Simmonite, W. J. *Horary Astrology: The Key to Scientific Prediction, being the prognostic astronomer. With additions by J. Story and further edited in the light of American experience by E. A. Grant*. Tempe, AZ: The American Federation of Astrologers, 1950.

Titsworth, Joan, T. *Case Studies in Horary Astrology*. Venice, CA: Astro-Analytics, 1975.

Venker, J. *Astrowatch*. Deventer, Holland: Ankh-Hermes, 1980.

deVore, N. *Encyclopedia of Astrology*, Totowa, NJ: Littlefield, Adams & Co., 1976.

Watters, Barbara. *Horary Astrology and the Judgement of Events*. Washington, DC: Valhalla, 1973.

Wilson, J. *A Complete Dictionary of Astrology*. New York: Samuel Weiser, 1974. Now out of print.

Zain, C. C. *Horary Astrology, Course VIII*. Los Angeles: Church of Light, 1973.

Index

Karen Hamaker-Zondag is one of the leading members of the Astrological Foundation, *Arcturus*, in Holland. She is a graduate of the University of Amsterdam with doctoral degrees in social geography and environmental engineering. Her post-graduate study of psychology, astrology, and parapsychology has inspired a counseling practice where she combines Jungian concepts with astrological theory. She is the author of *The Twelfth House, Aspects and Personality, Psychological Astrology, Elements and Crosses at the Basis of the Horoscope, Planetary Symbolism in the Horoscope,* and *Houses and Personality Development,* all published by Weiser. She has lectured extensively in Holland, Belgium, Germany, England, the United States of America, Switzerland, Scandinavia, and Canada, and most recently lectured at the United Astrology Congress (UAC) in Washington, DC.